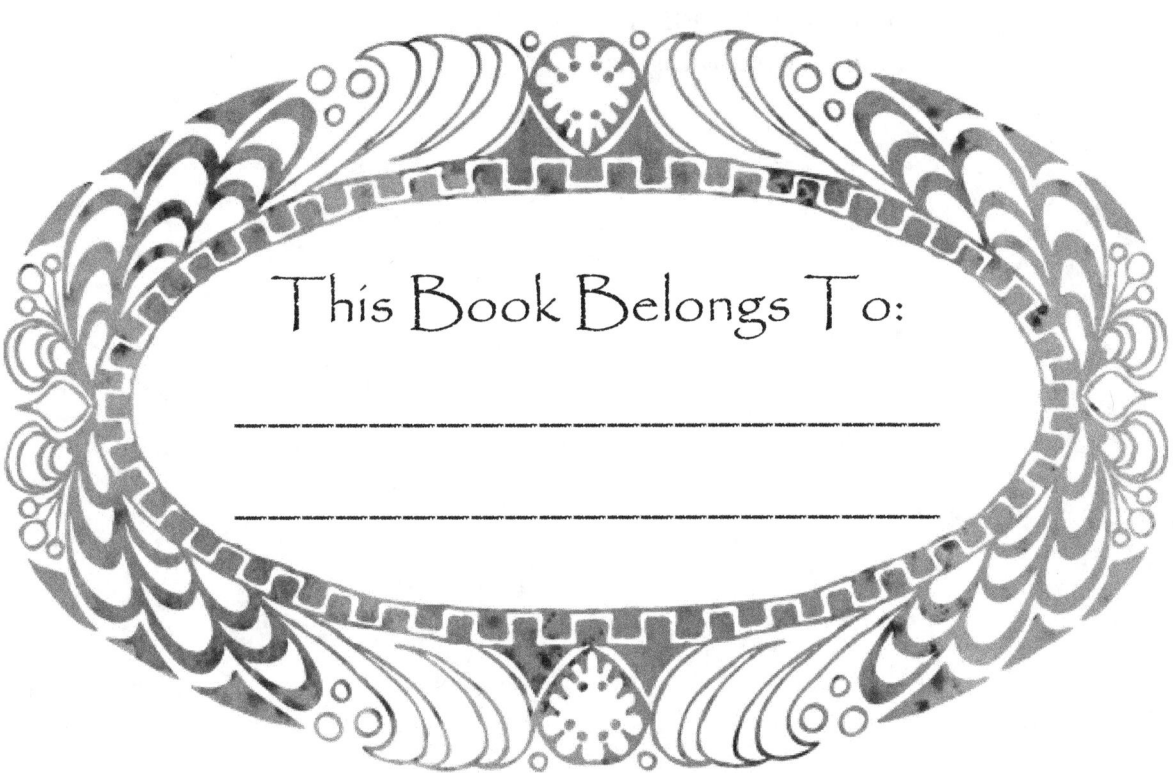

BlueMoon Paradigm, would love to hear from you - here's how you can reach us:

Web: www.bluemoonparadigm.com
Blog: bluemoonparadigm.blogspot.com
Email: bluemoonparadigm@gmail.com

Also:

 *coming soon!*

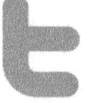 *coming soon!*

 *coming soon!*

Shop our journals, notebooks & more at:

www.bluemoonparadigm.com

Wholesale Info: www.bluemoonparadigm.com *for more details!*

For questions &
customer service,
email us at: *bluemoonparadigm@gmail.com*

© 2020 BlueMoon Paradigm. All rights reserved. No part of this publication may be reproduced, distributed, or transmitted, in any form or by any means, including photocopying, recording, or other electronic or mechanical methods, without prior written permission of the publisher, except in the case of brief quotations embodied in critical reviews and certain other non-commercial uses permitted by copyright laws.

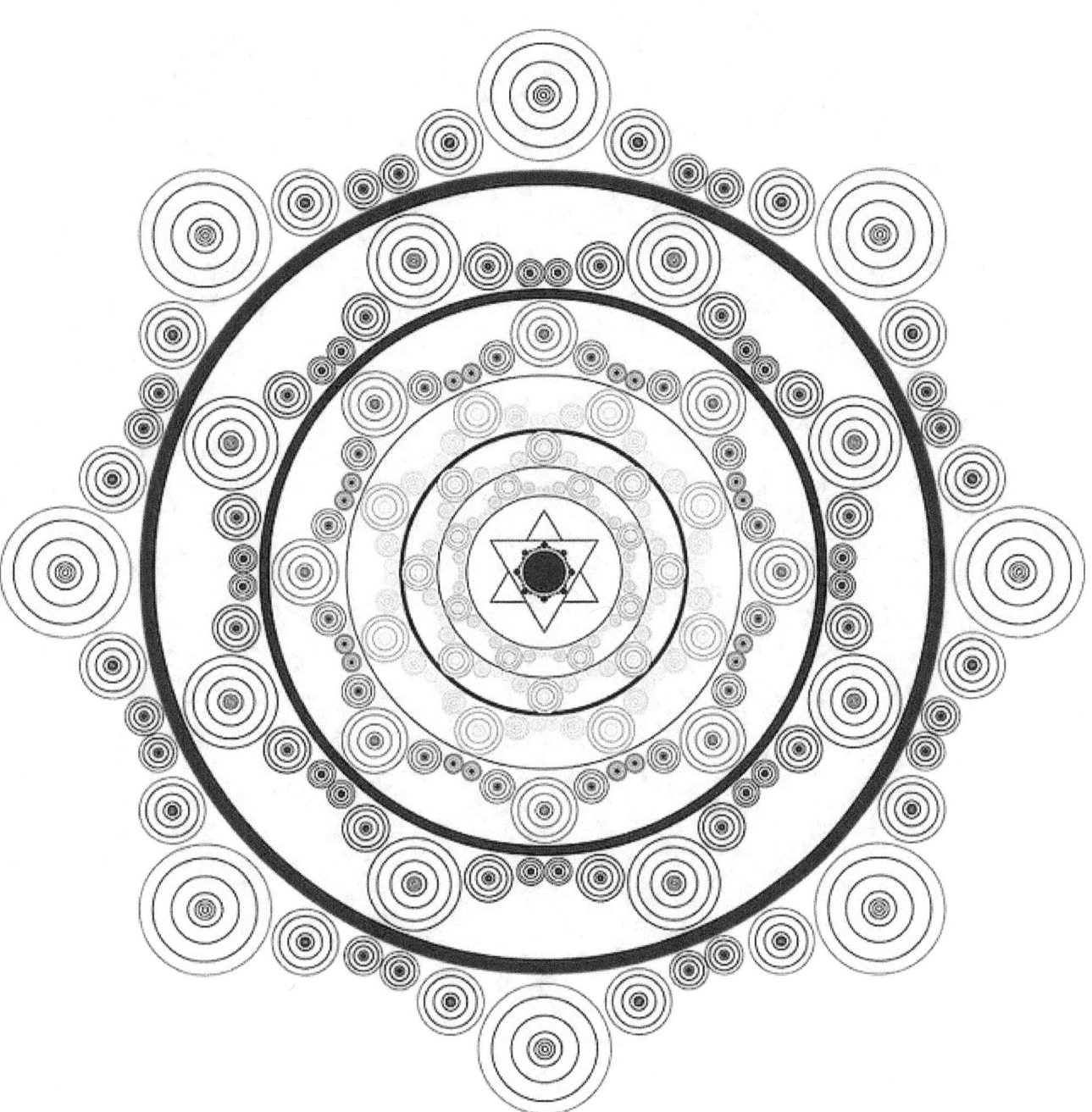

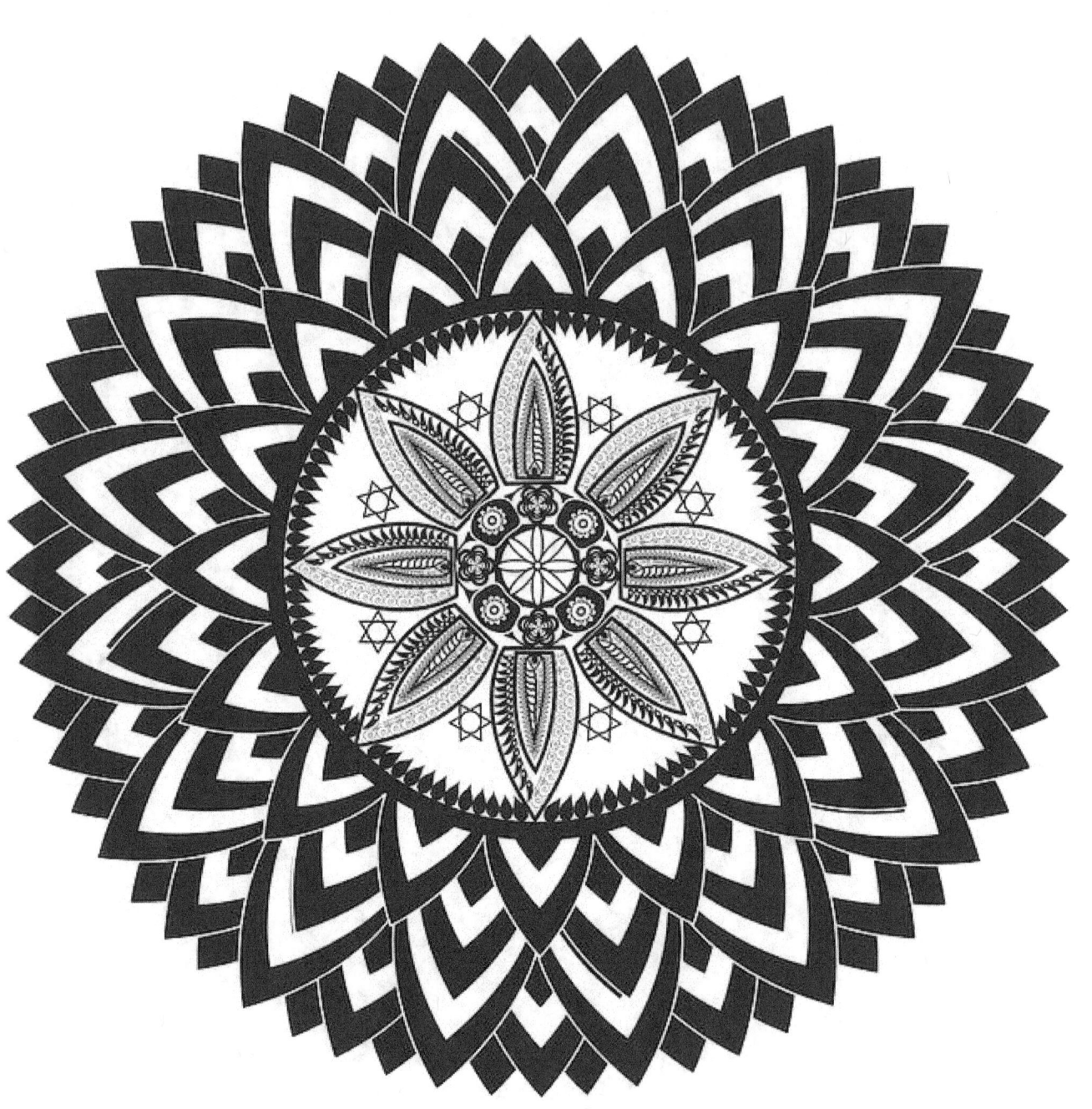

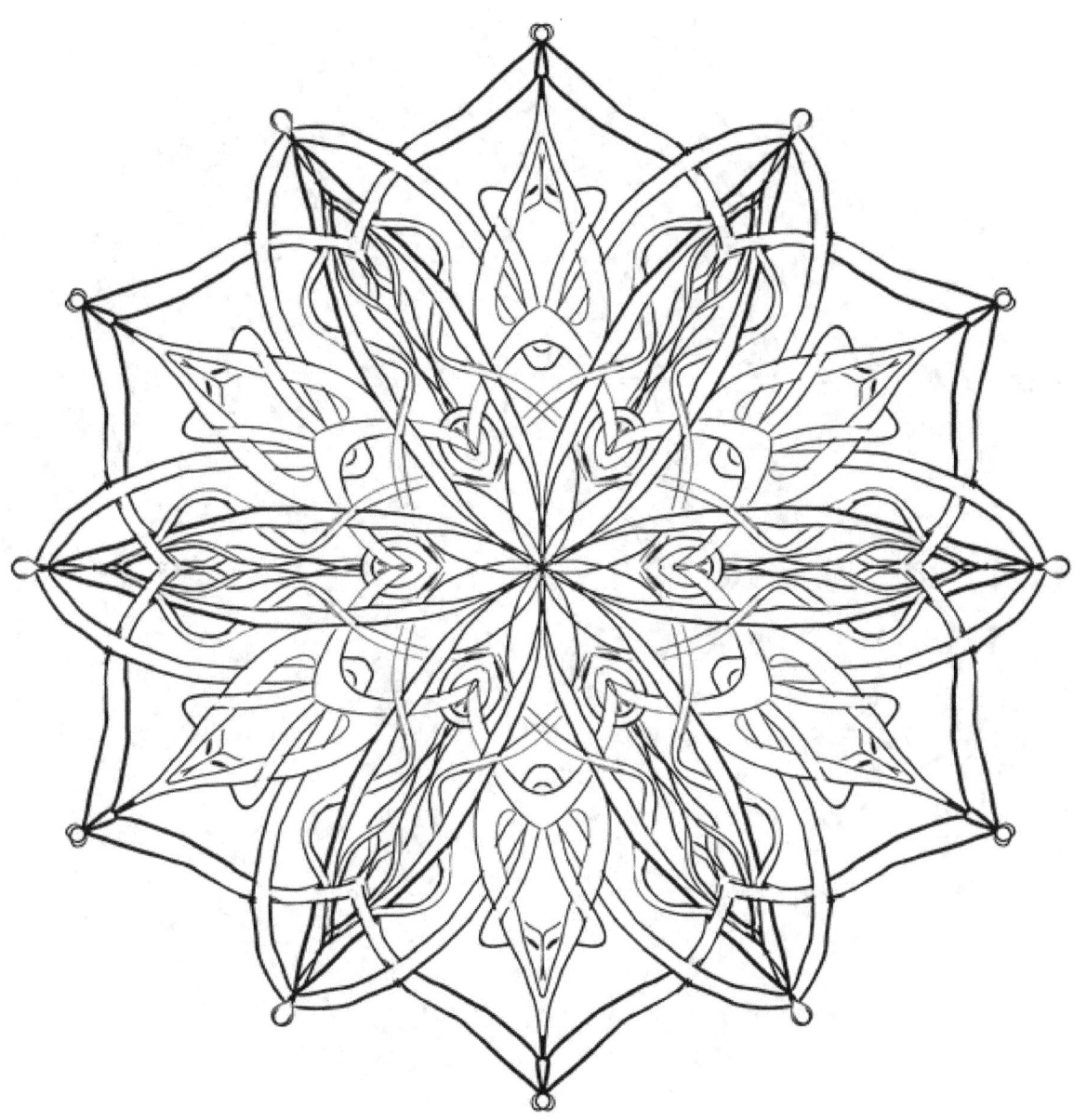

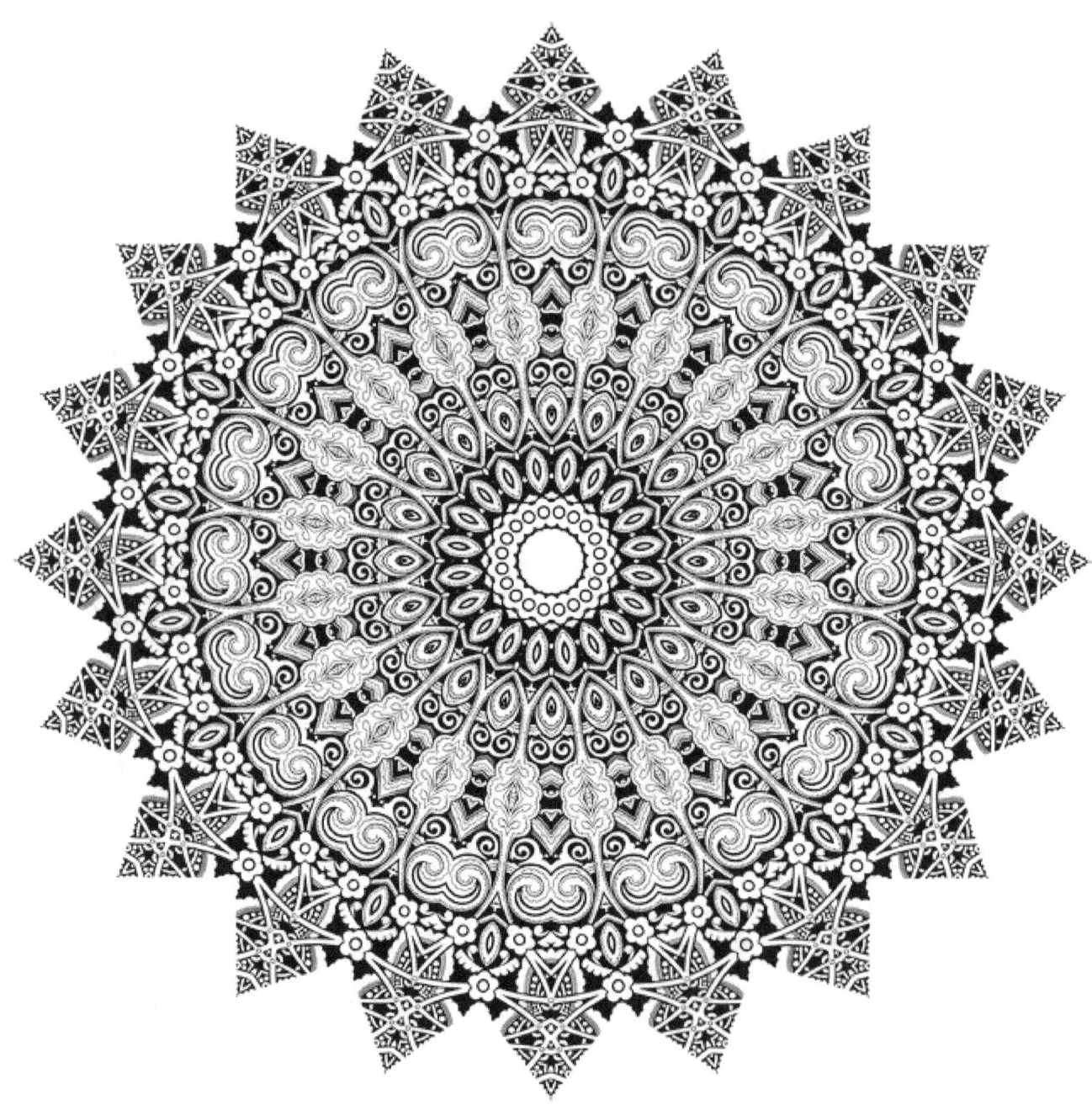

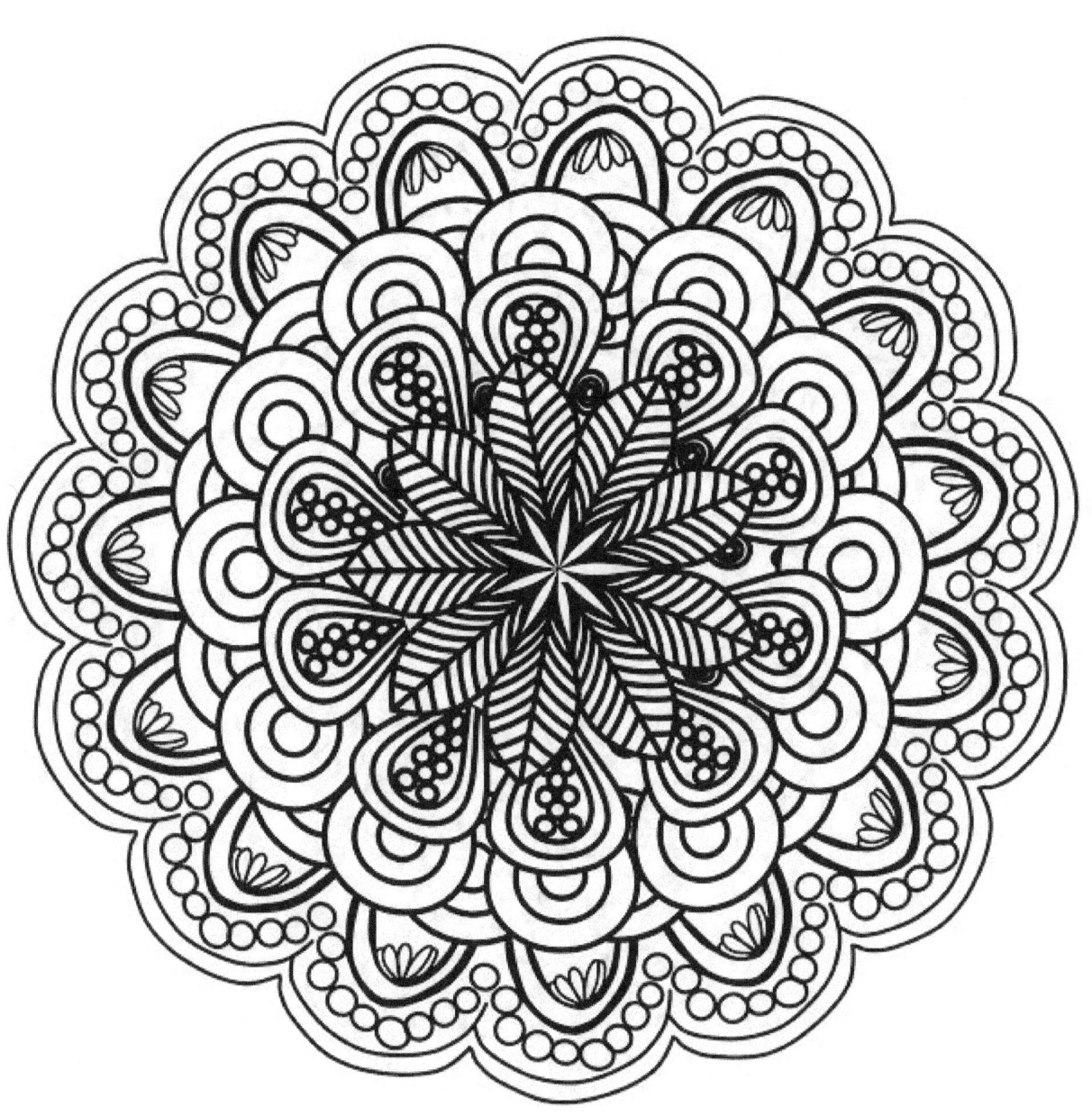

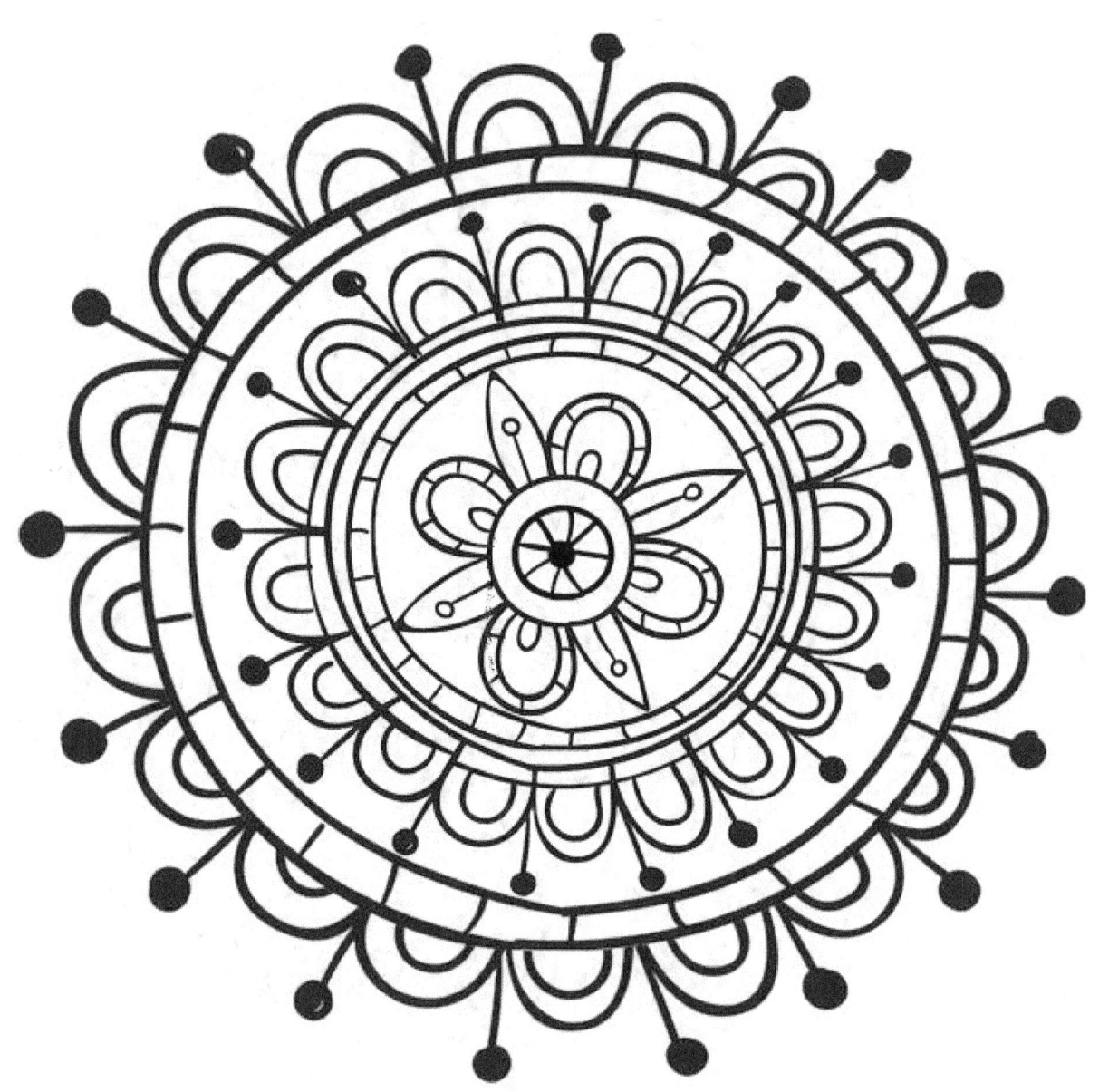

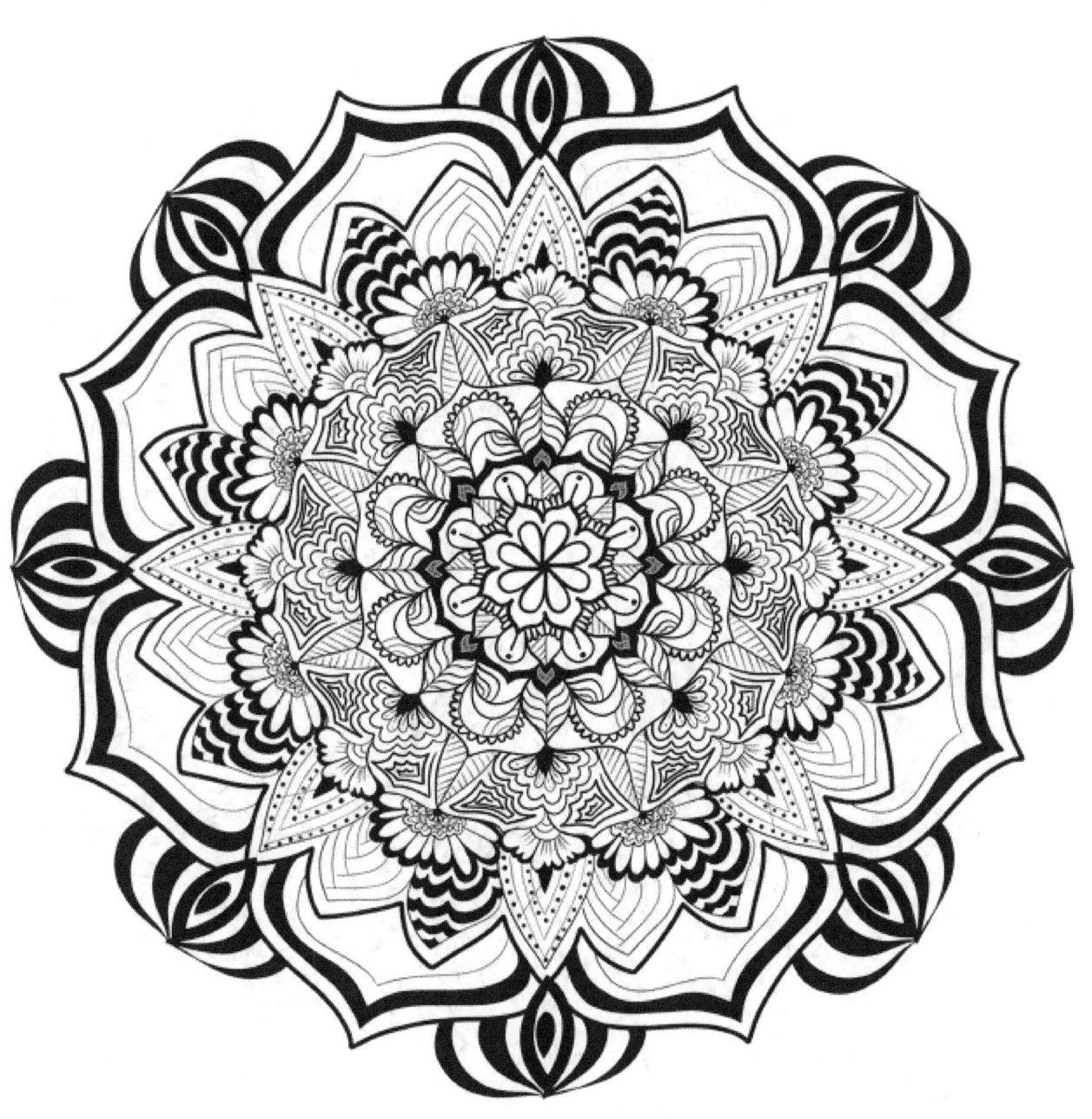

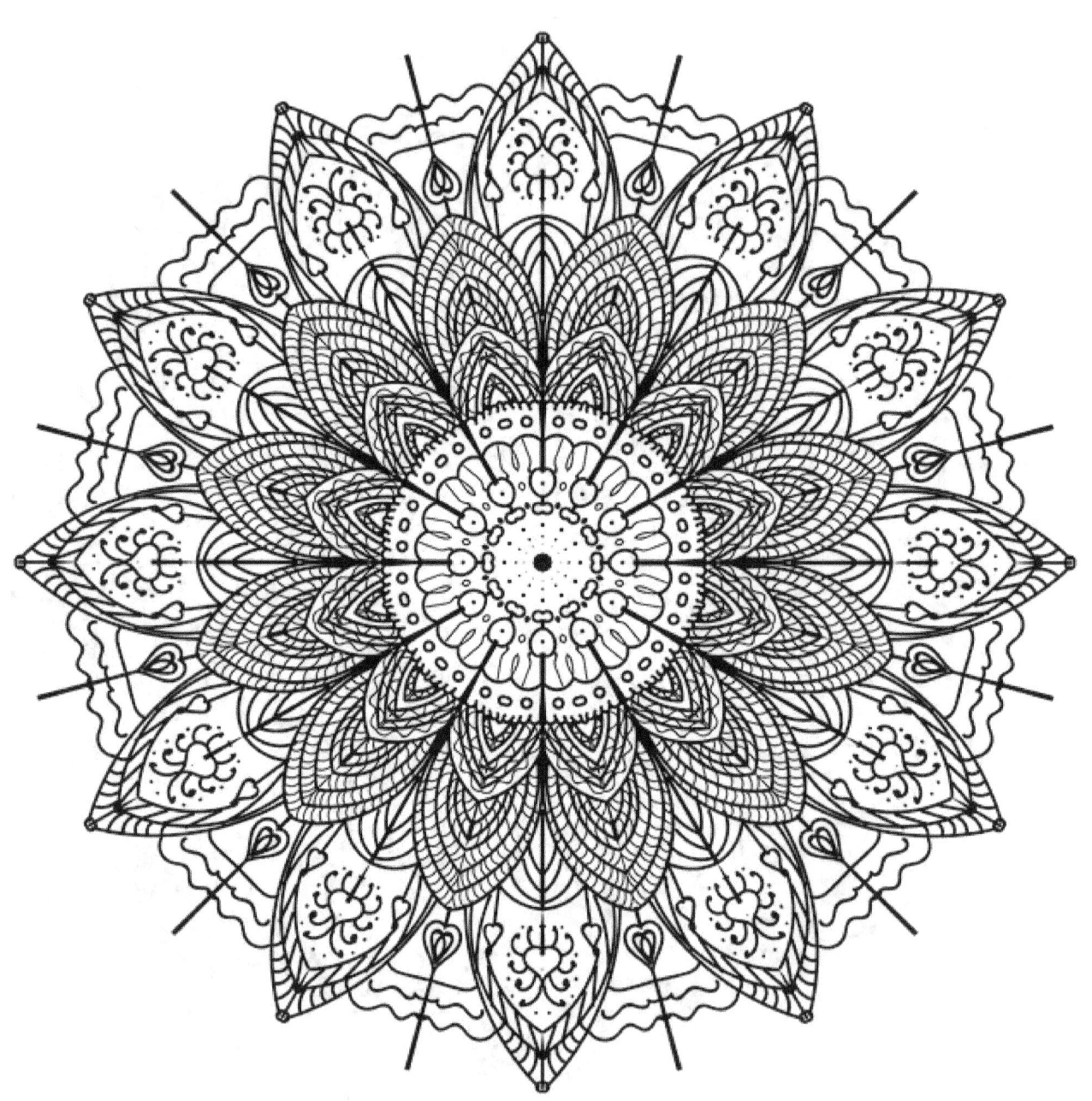

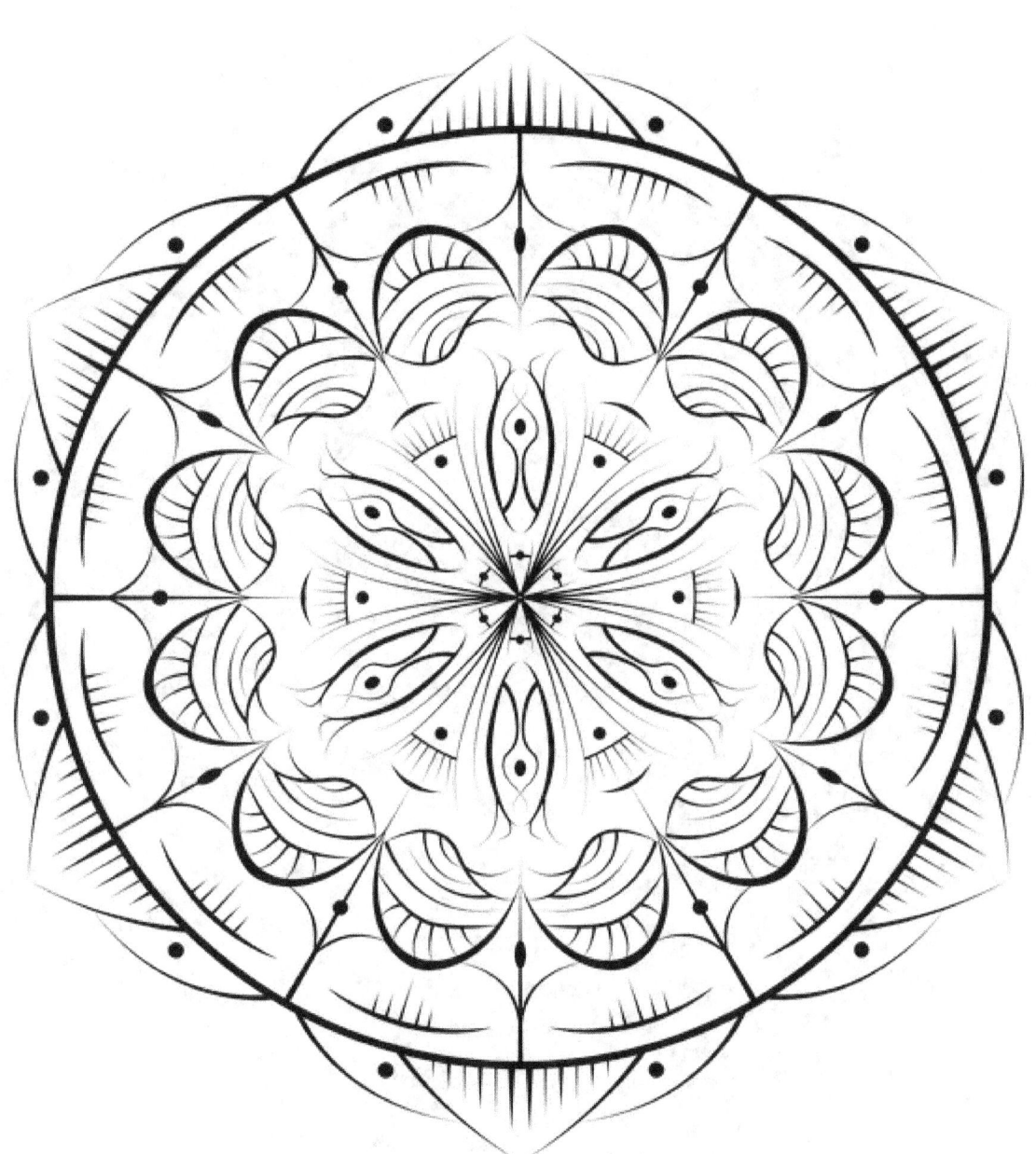

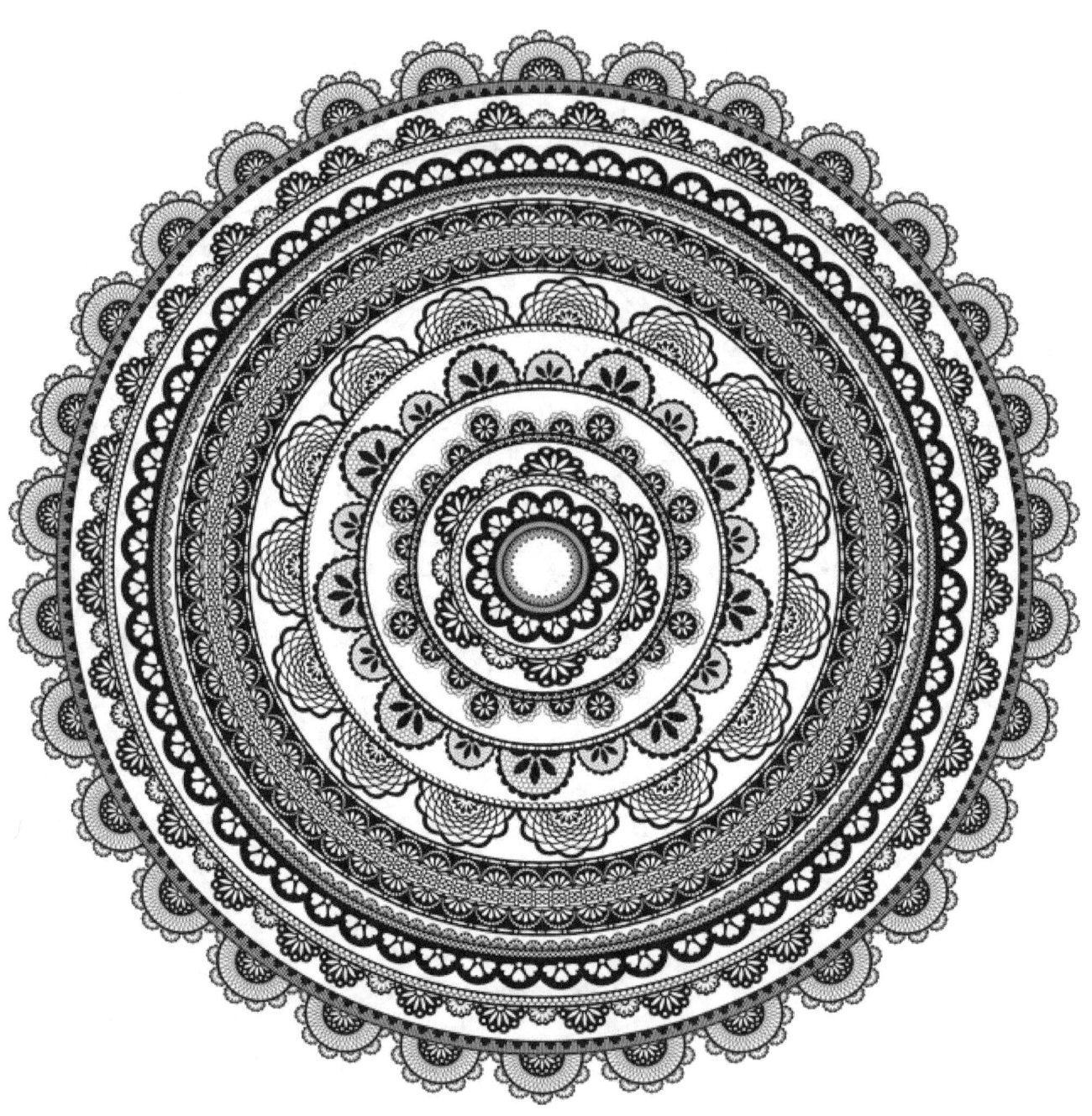

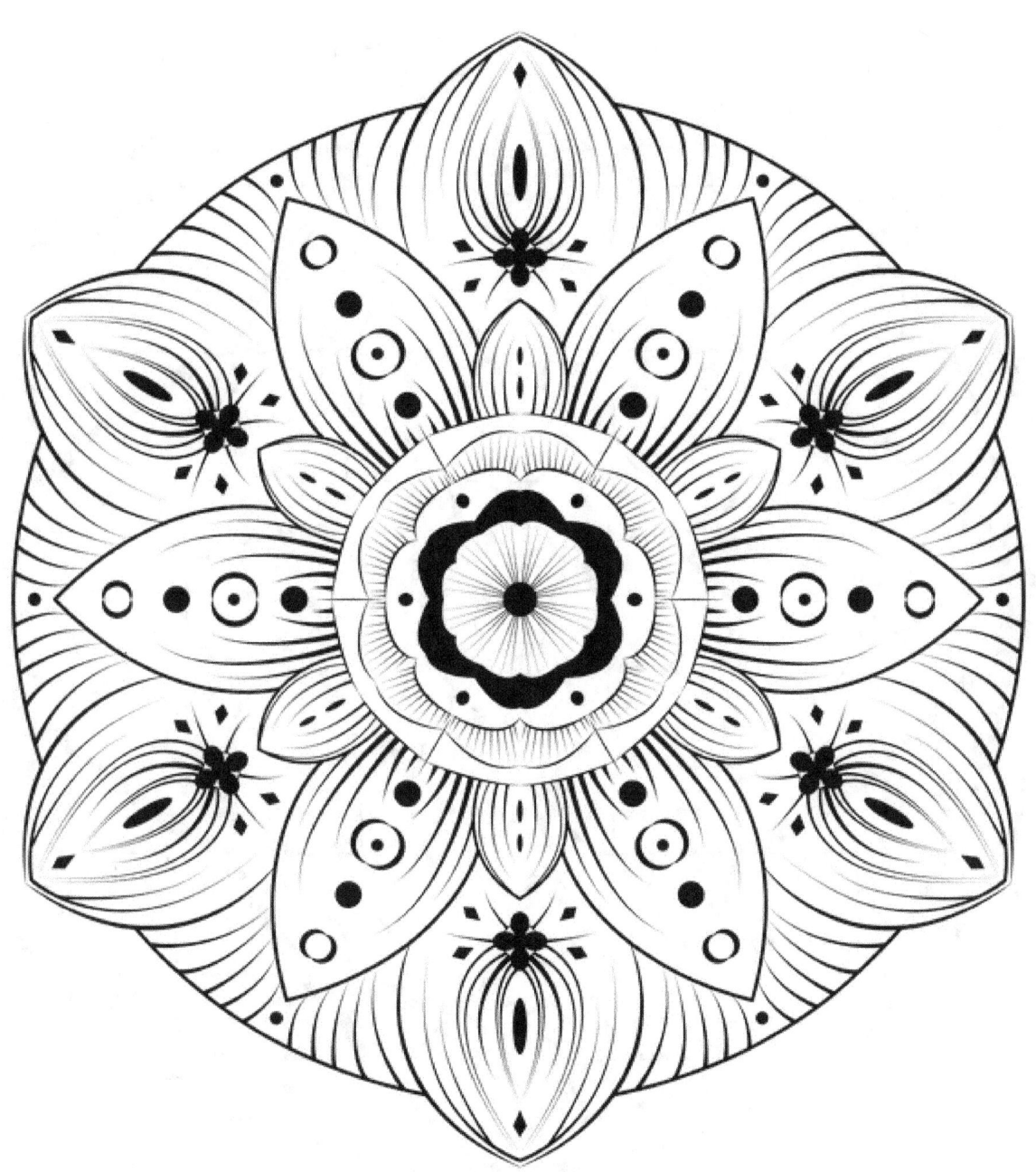

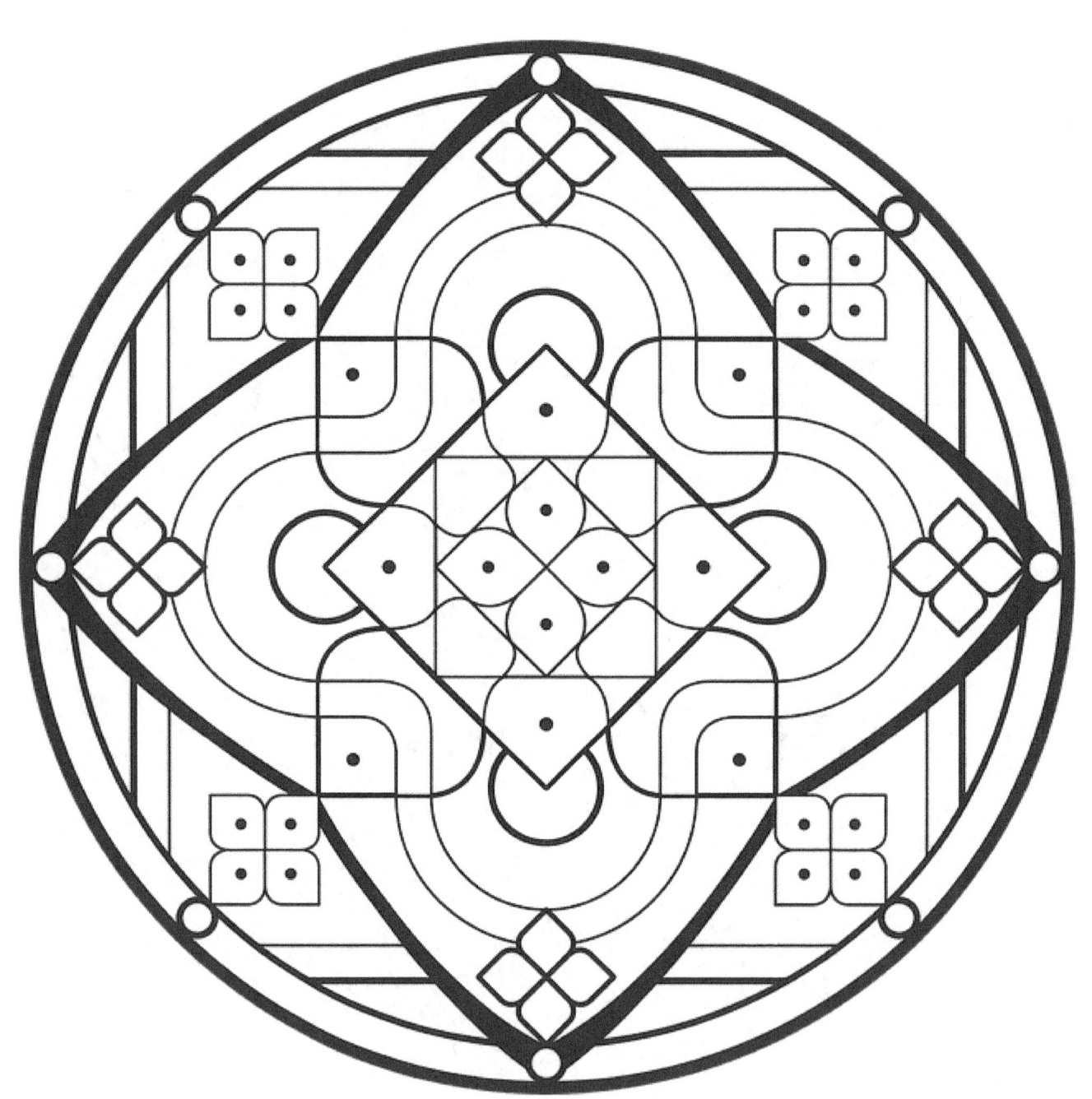

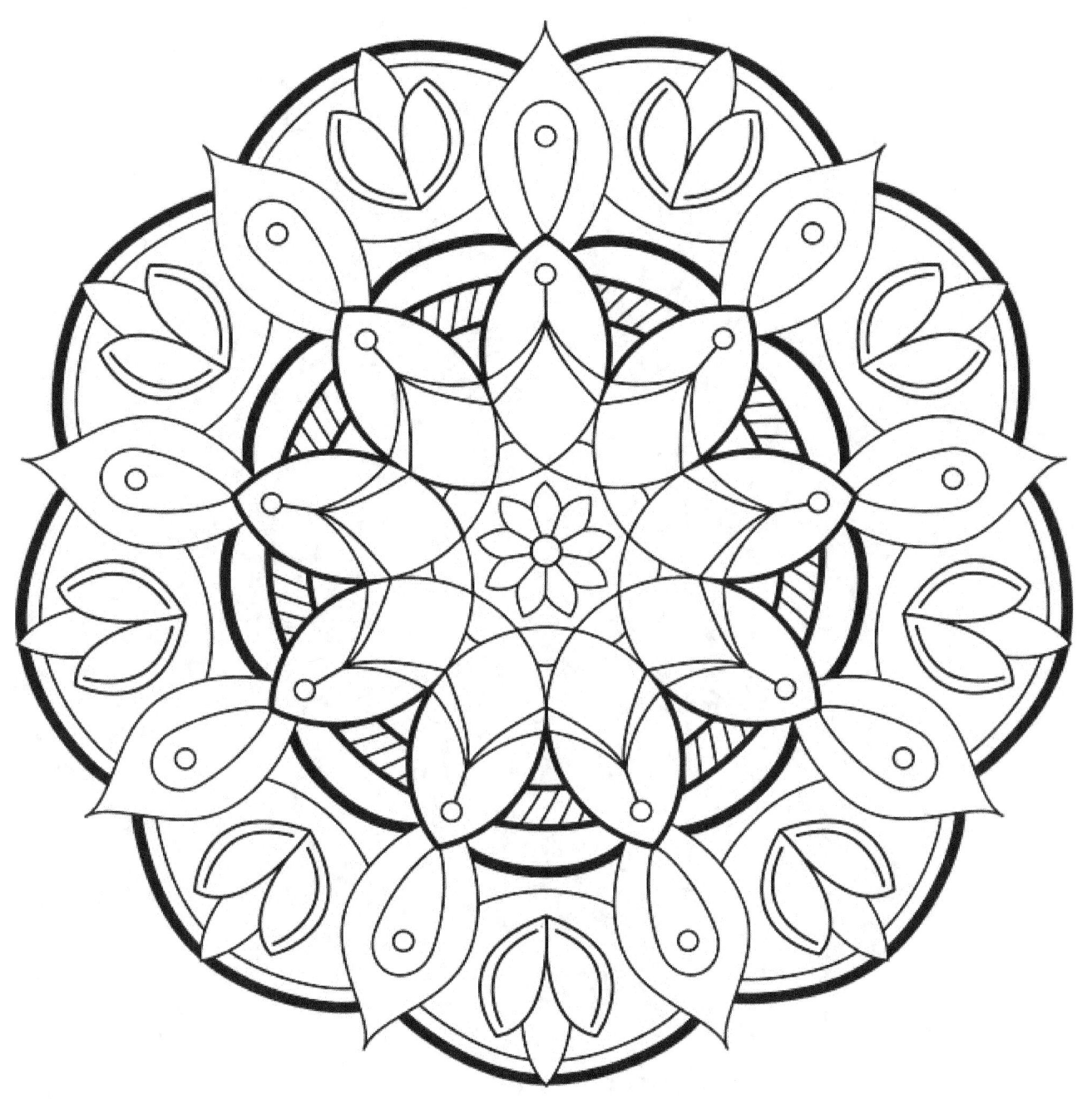

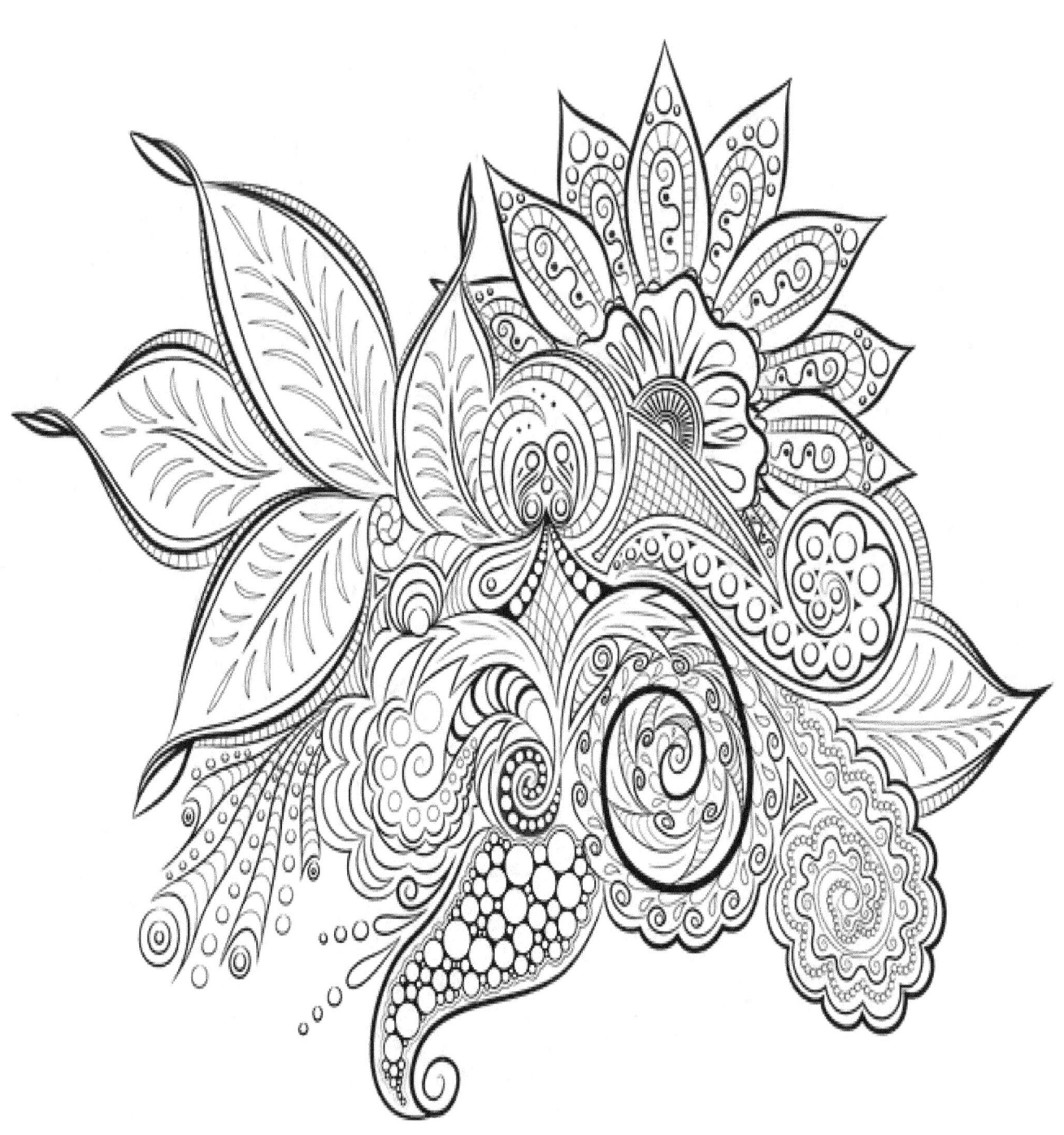

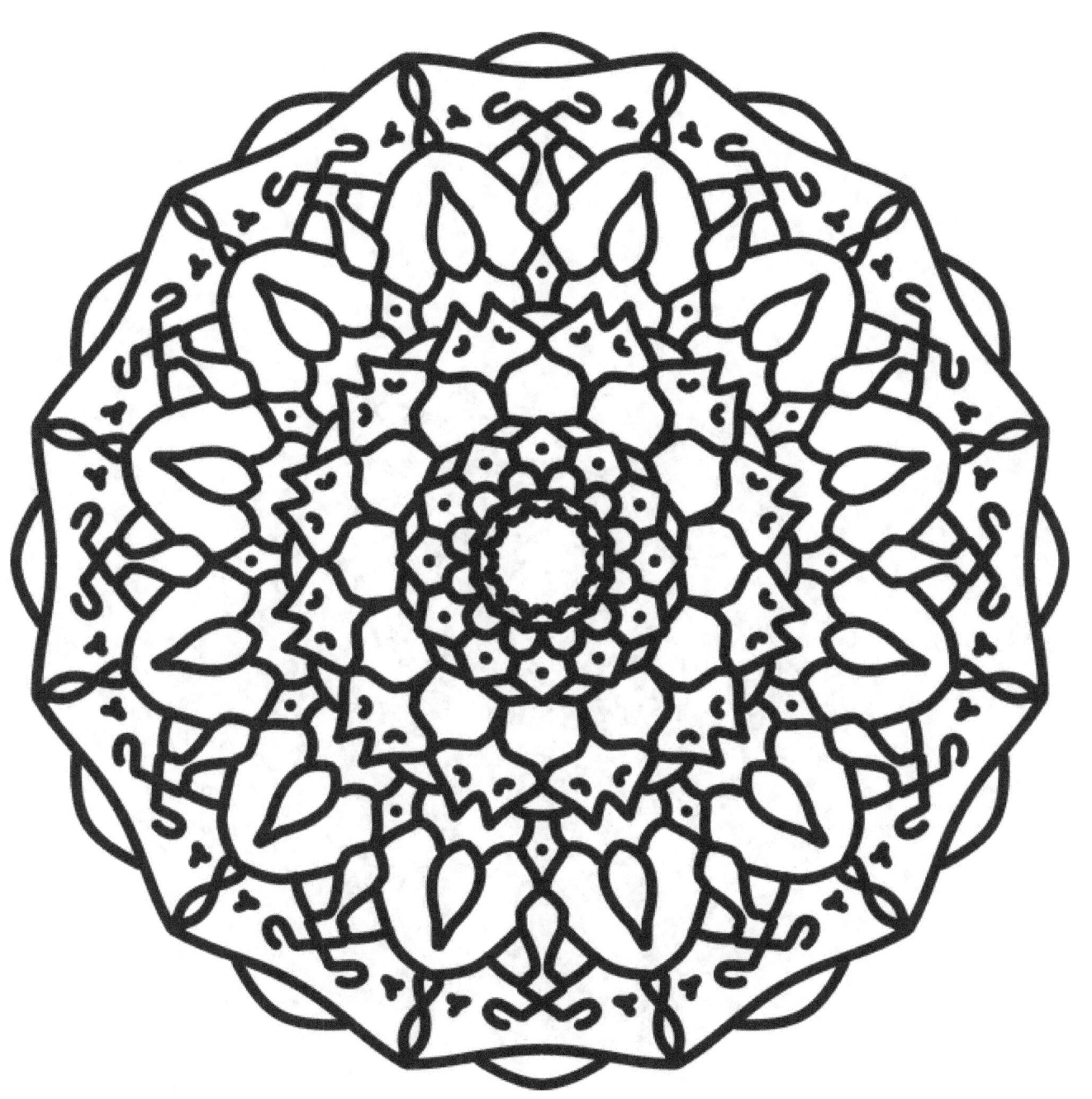

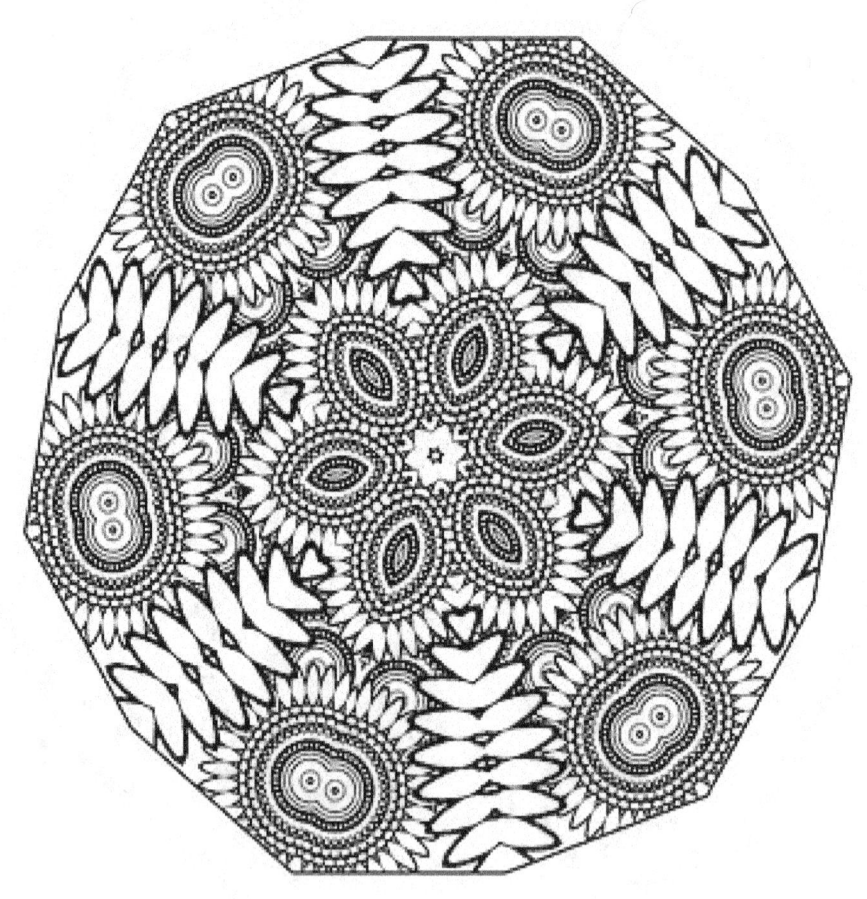

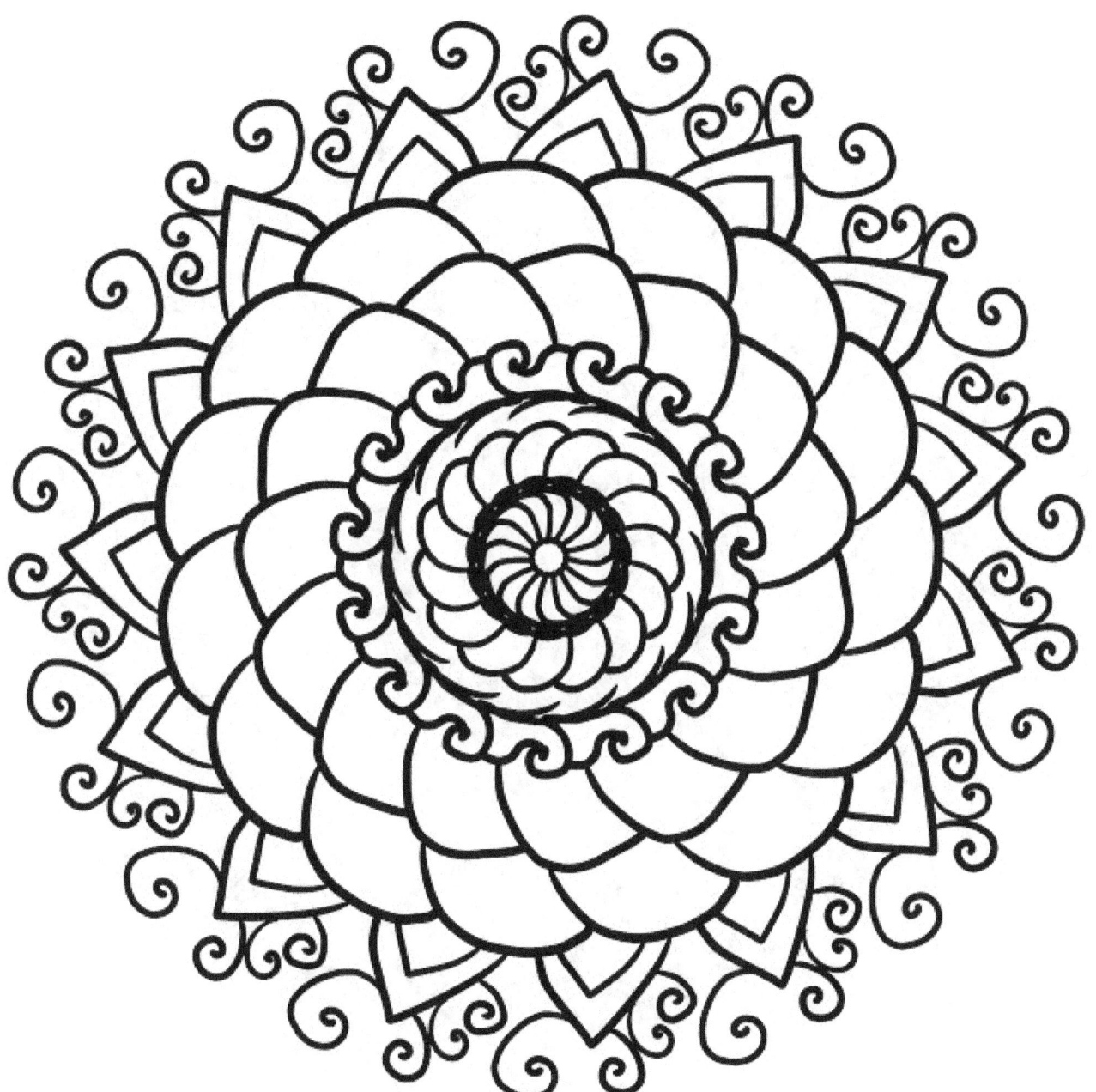

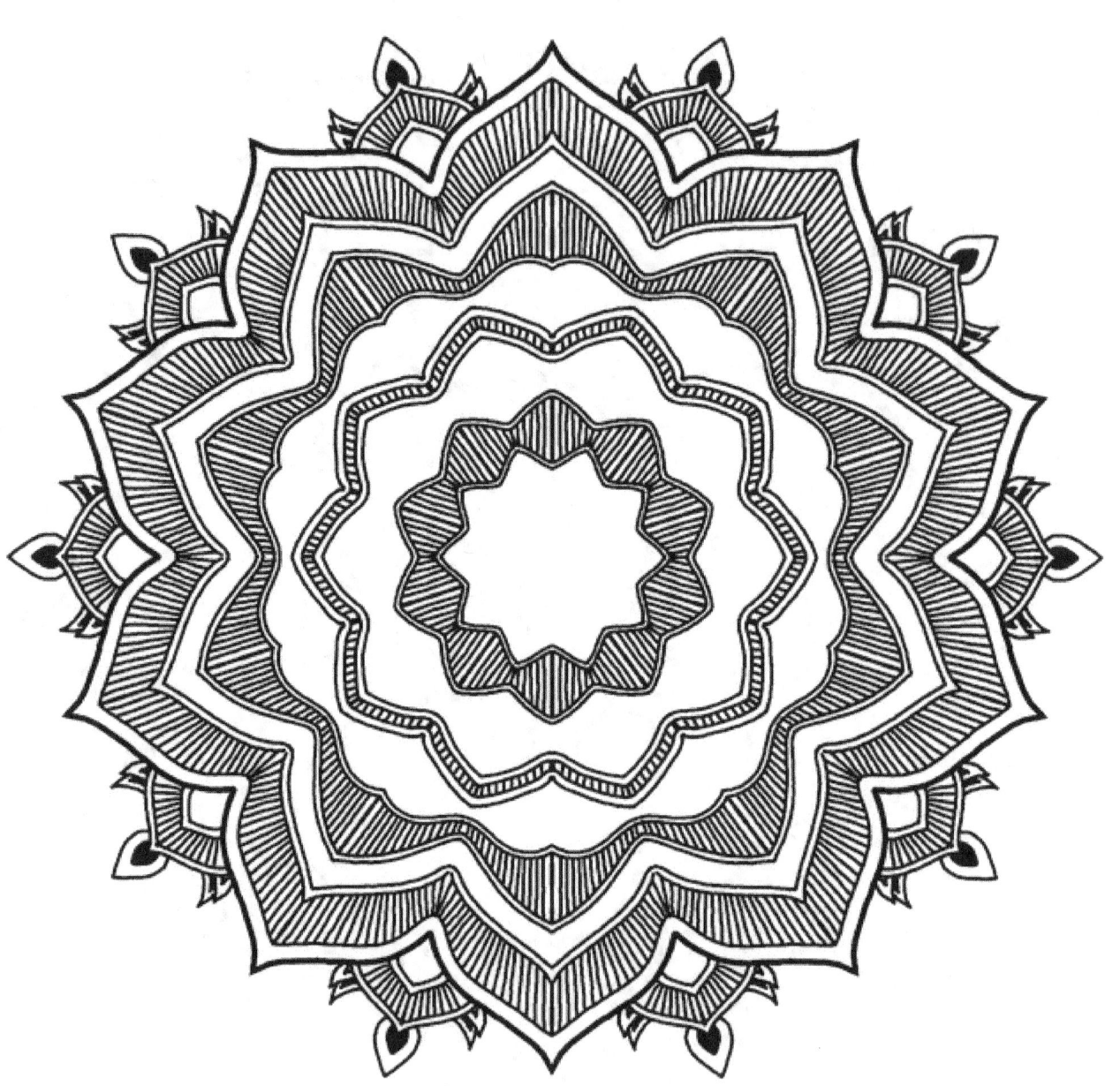

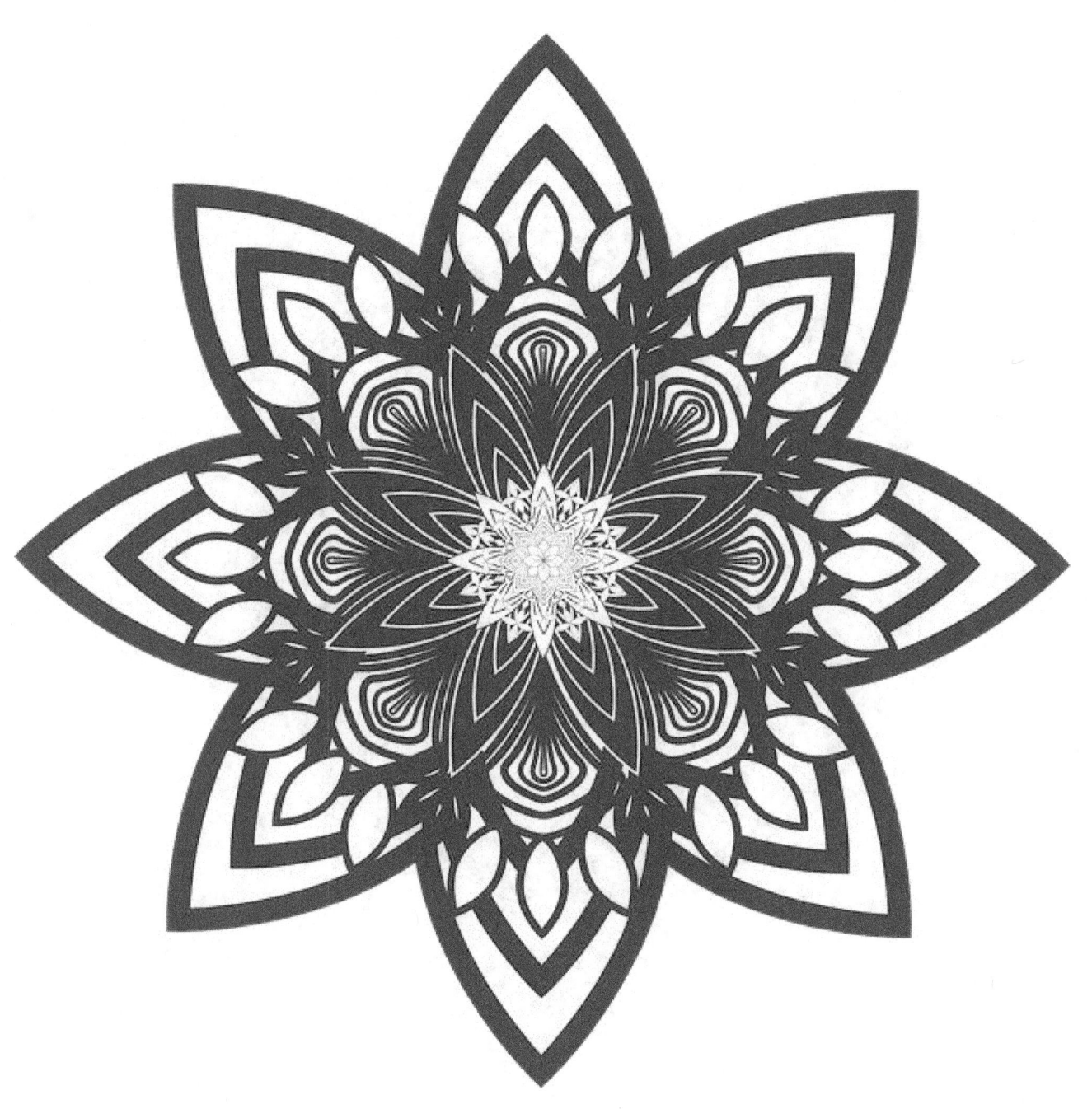

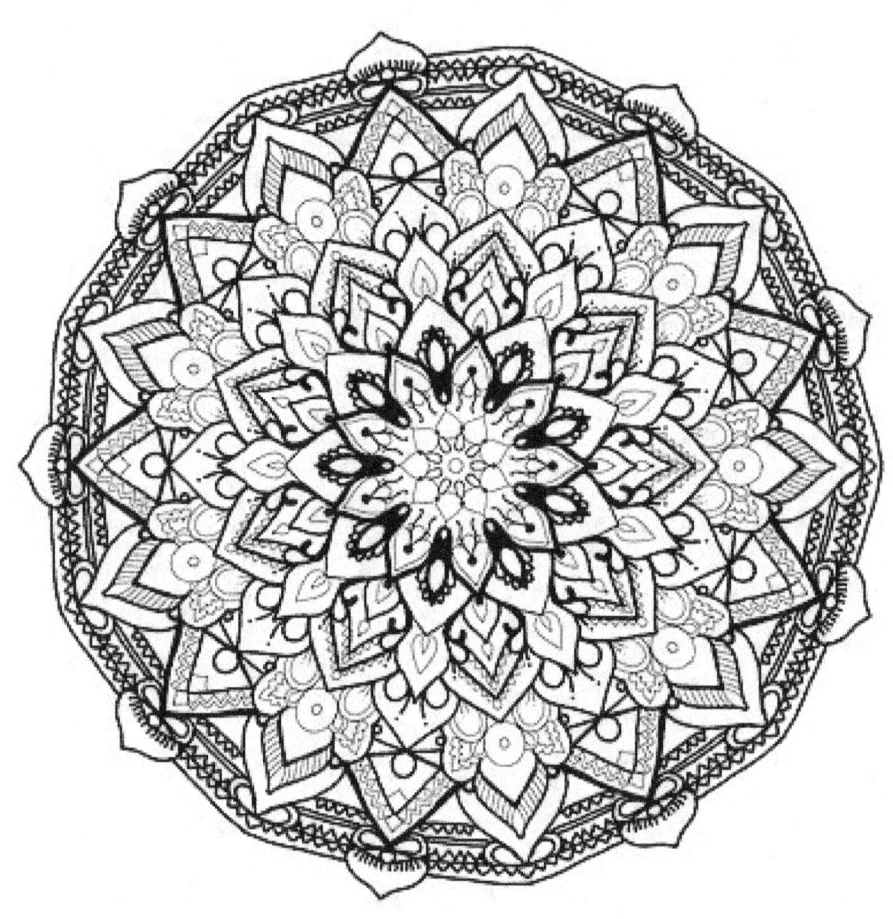

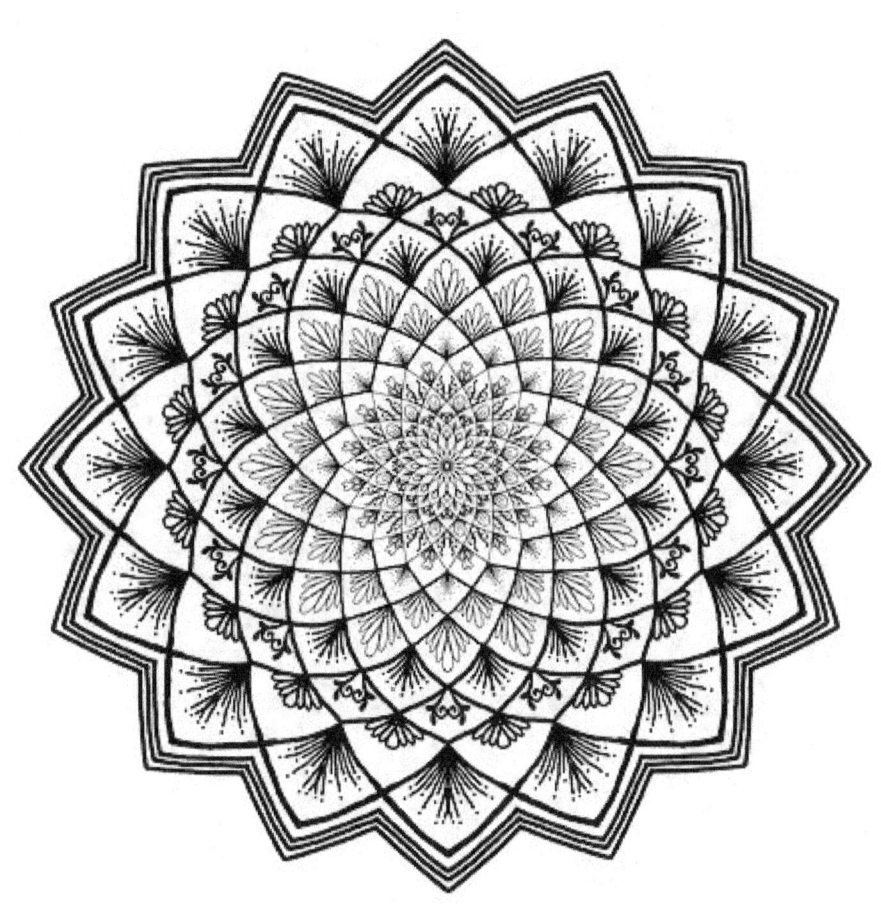

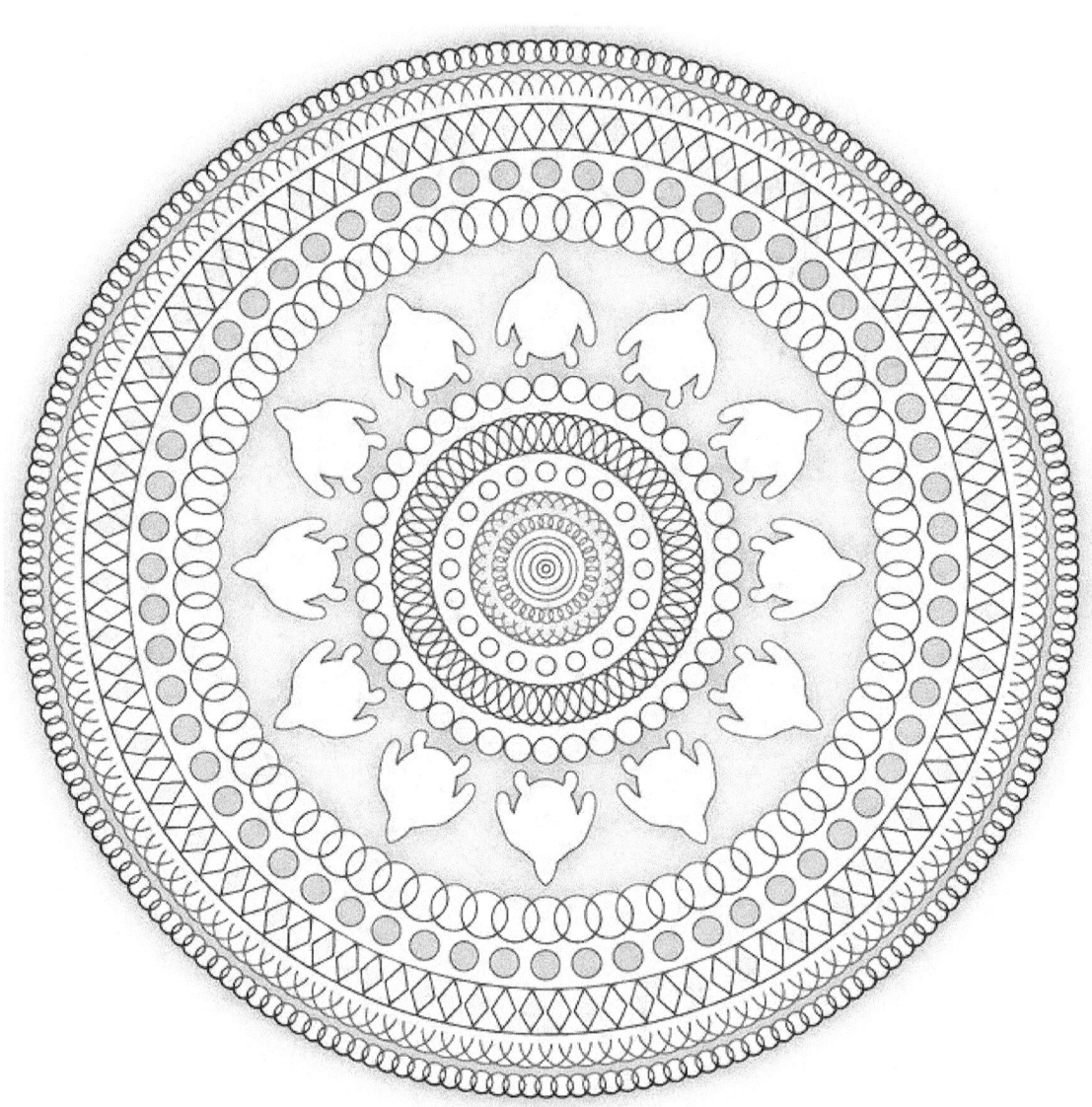

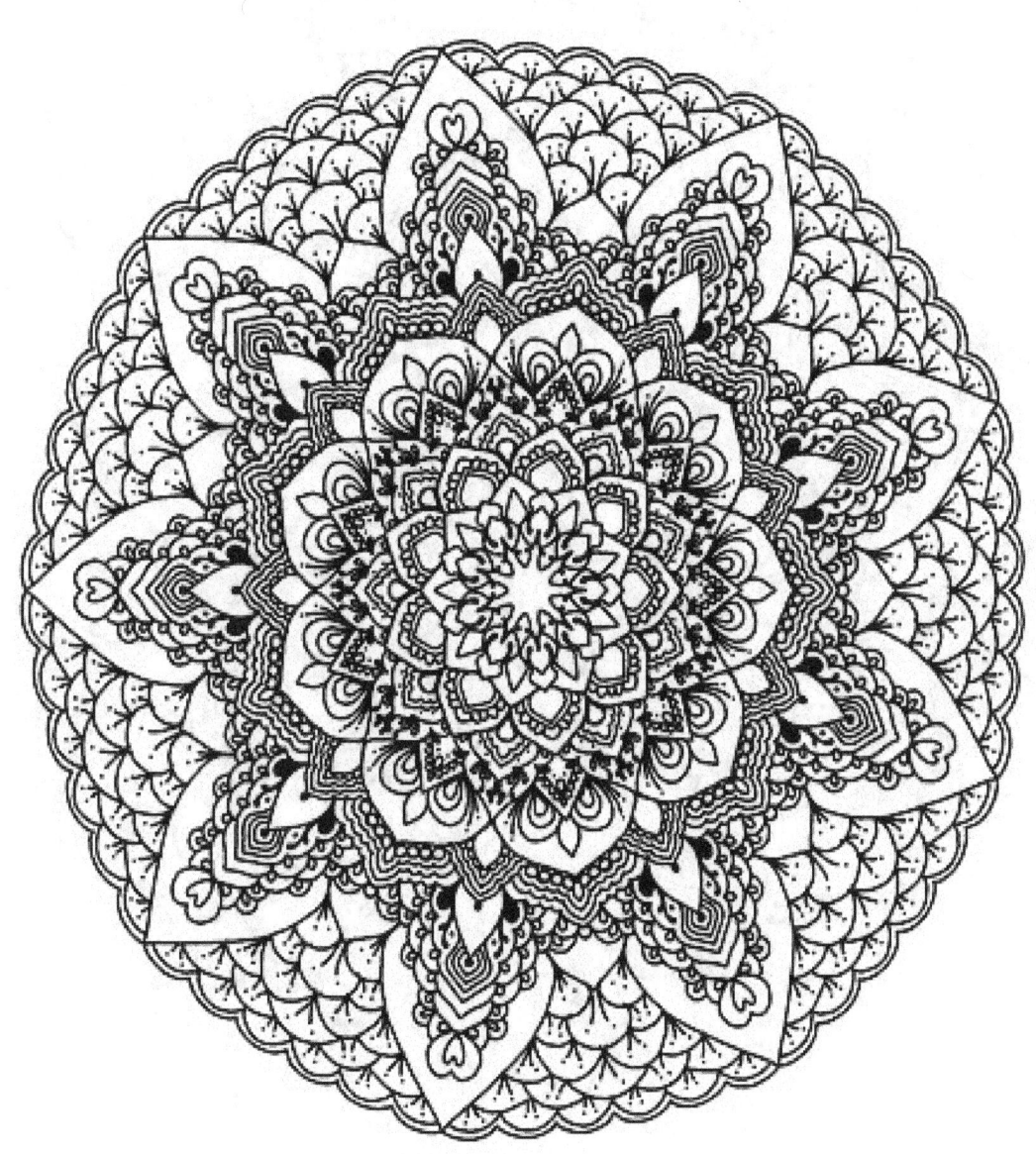

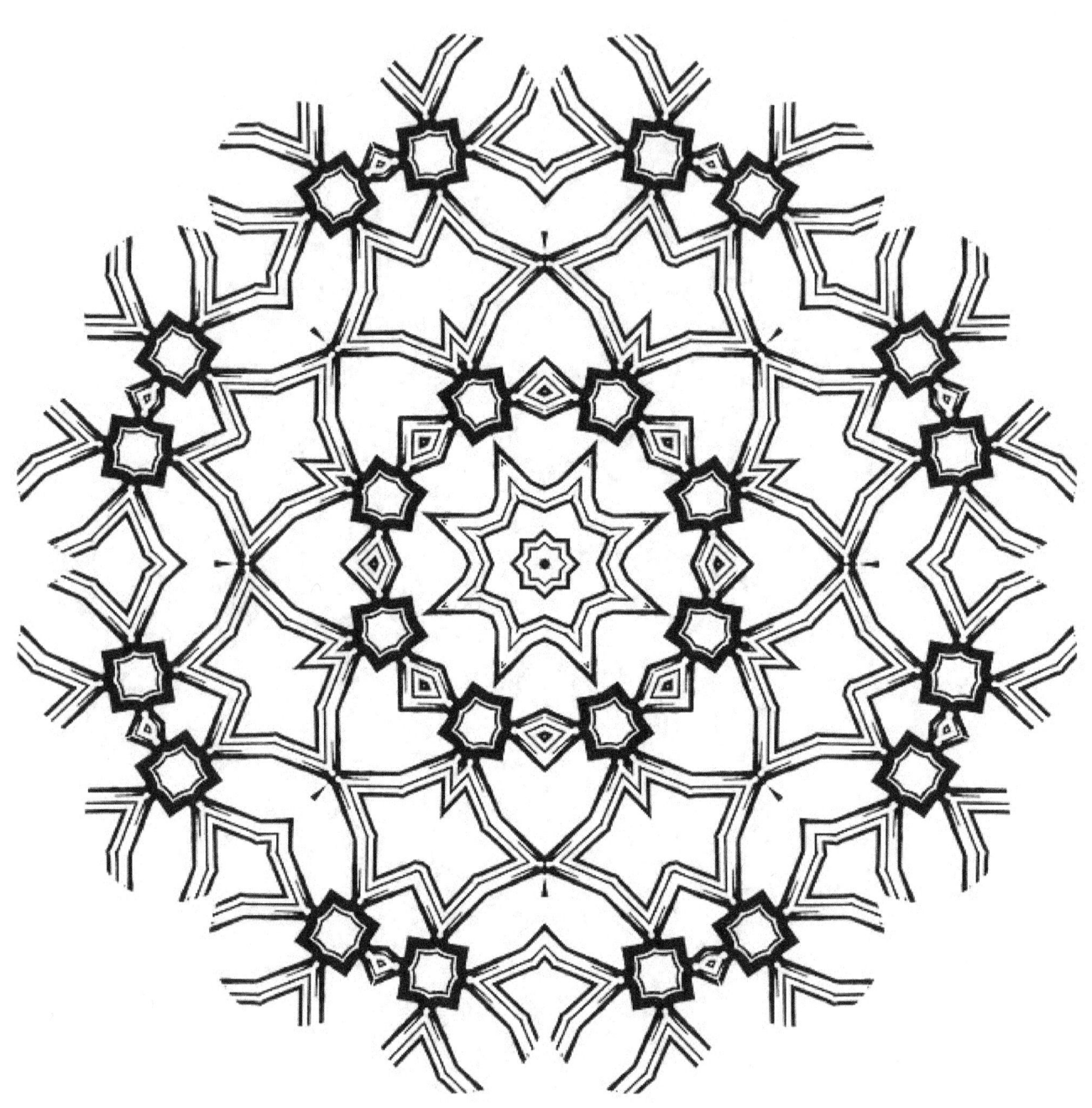

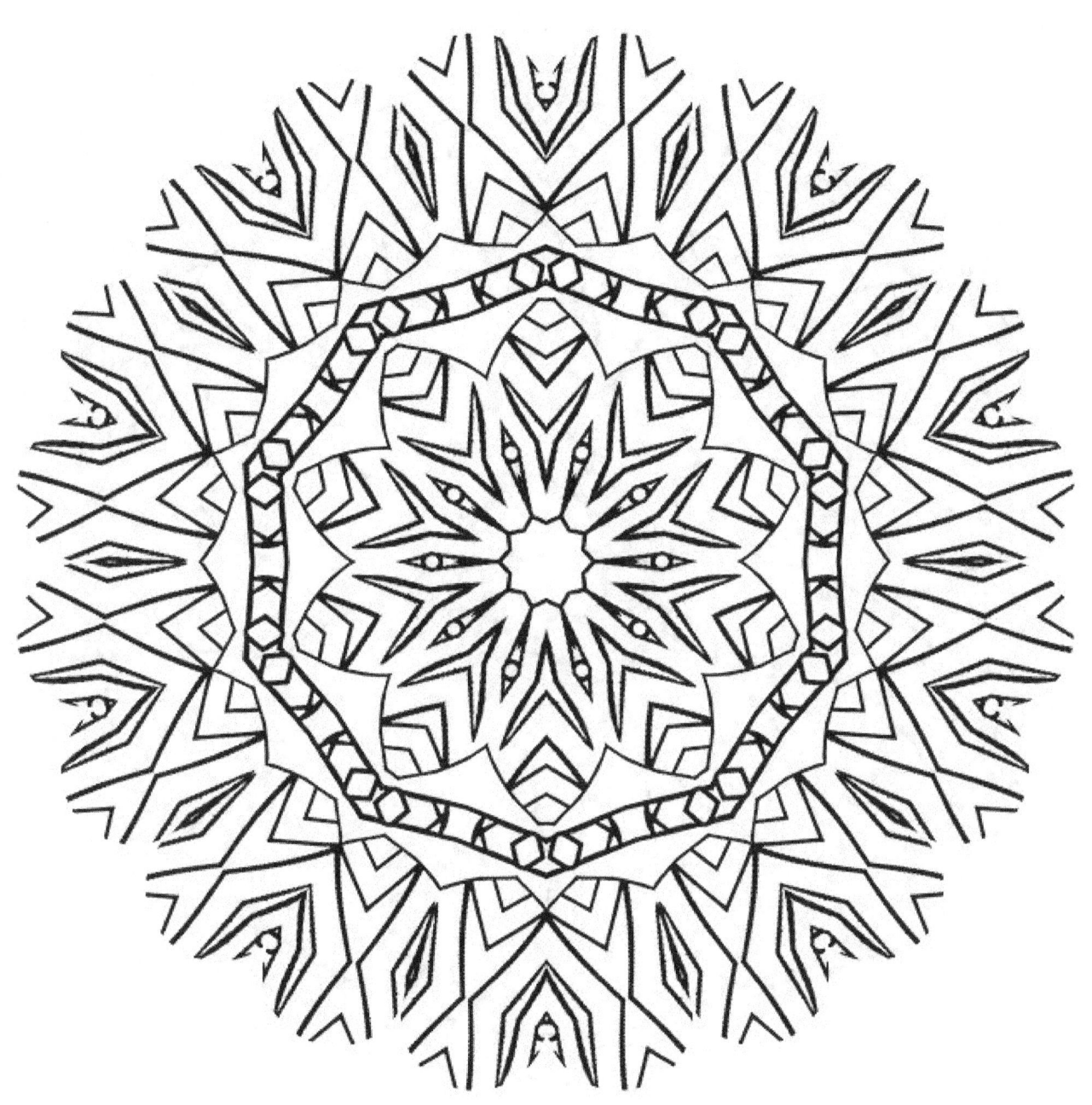

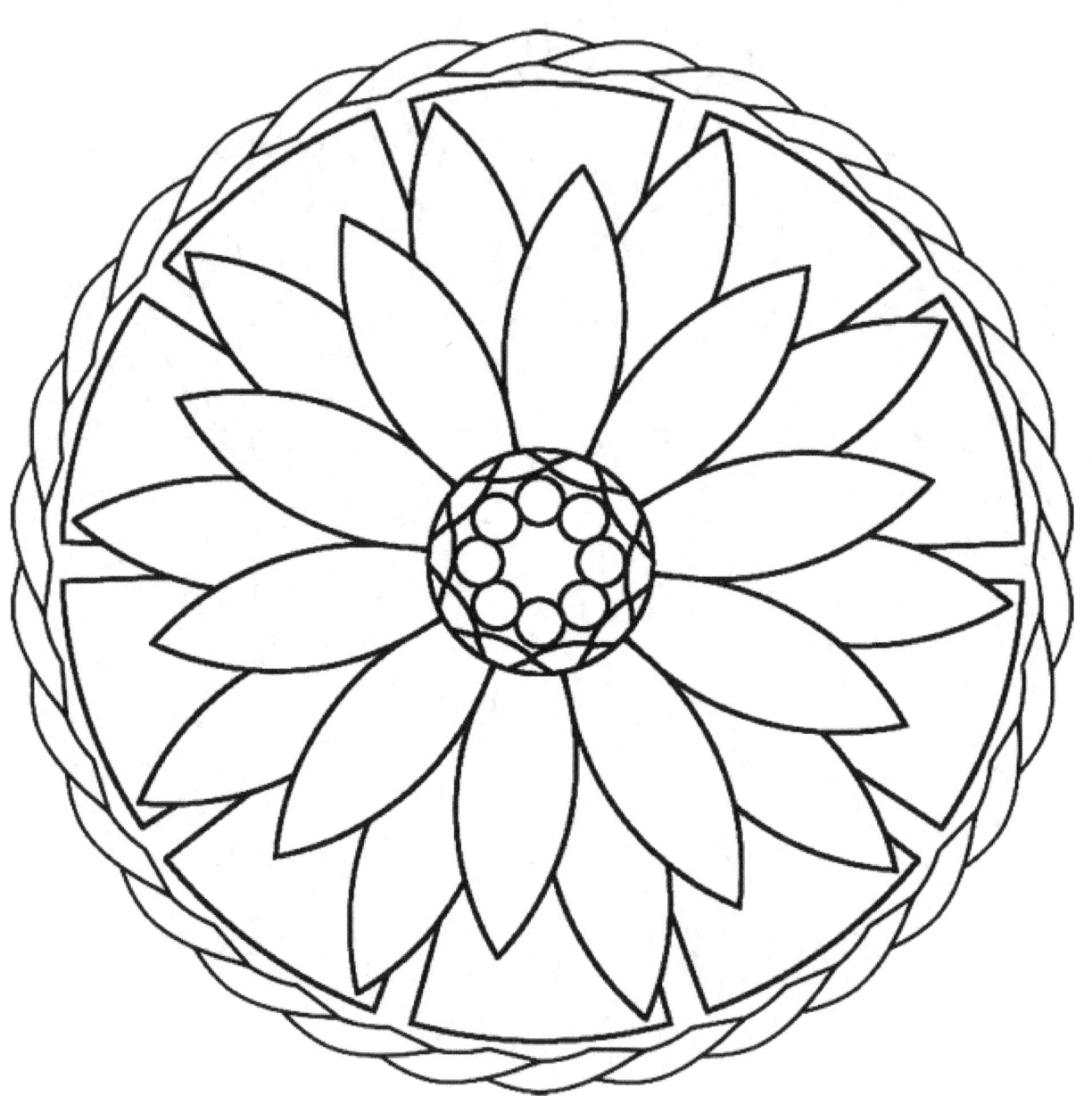

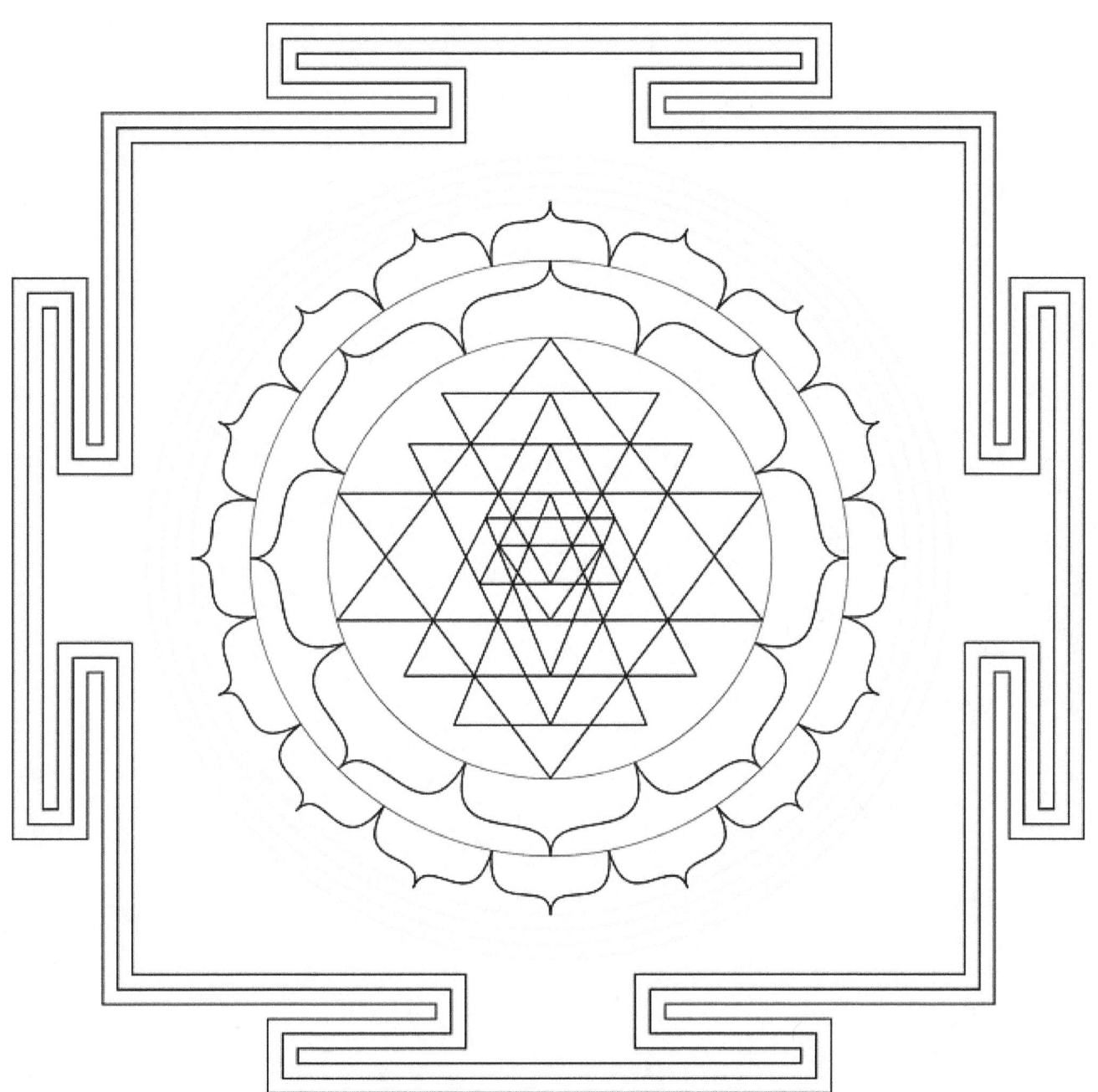

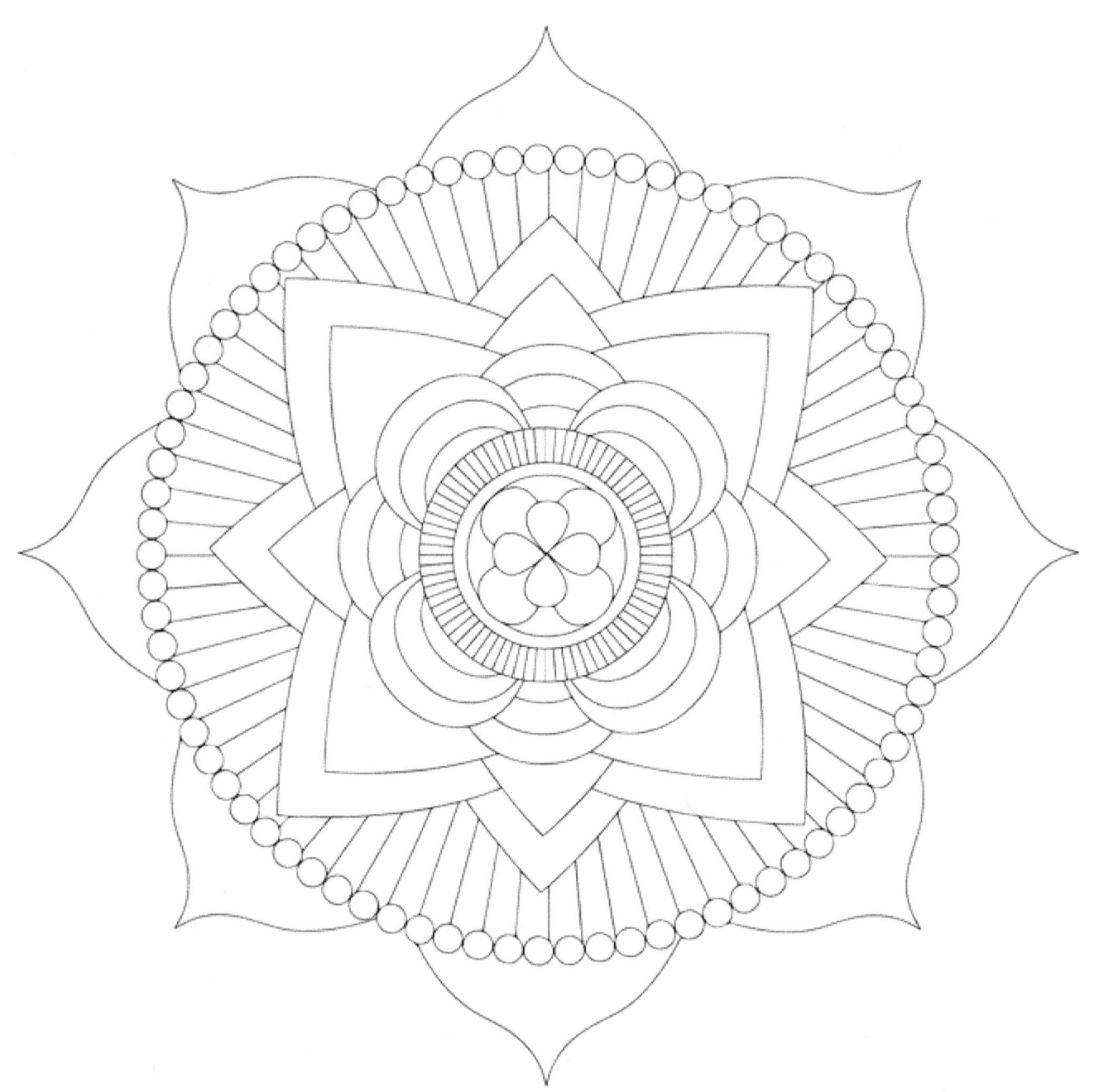

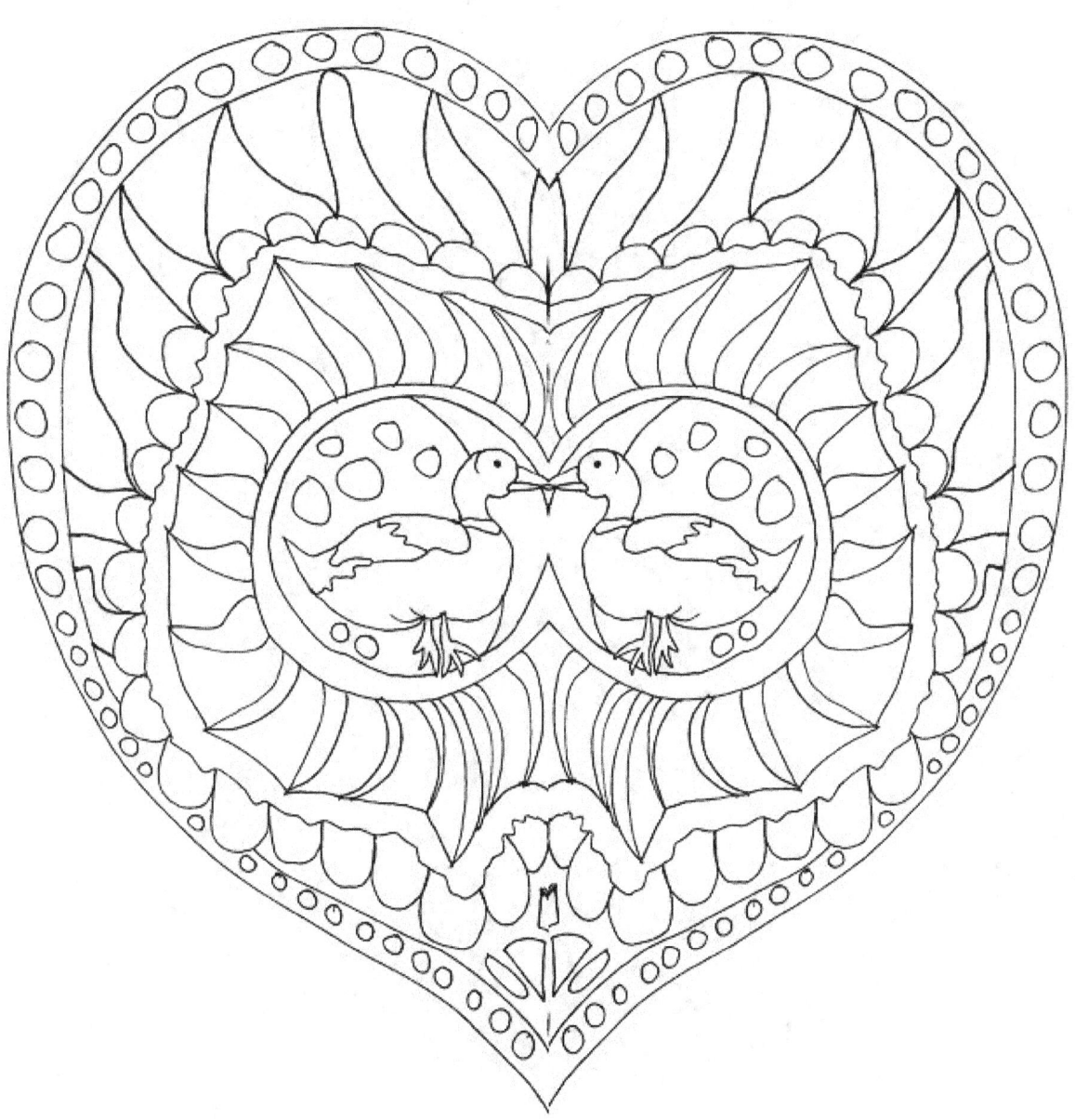

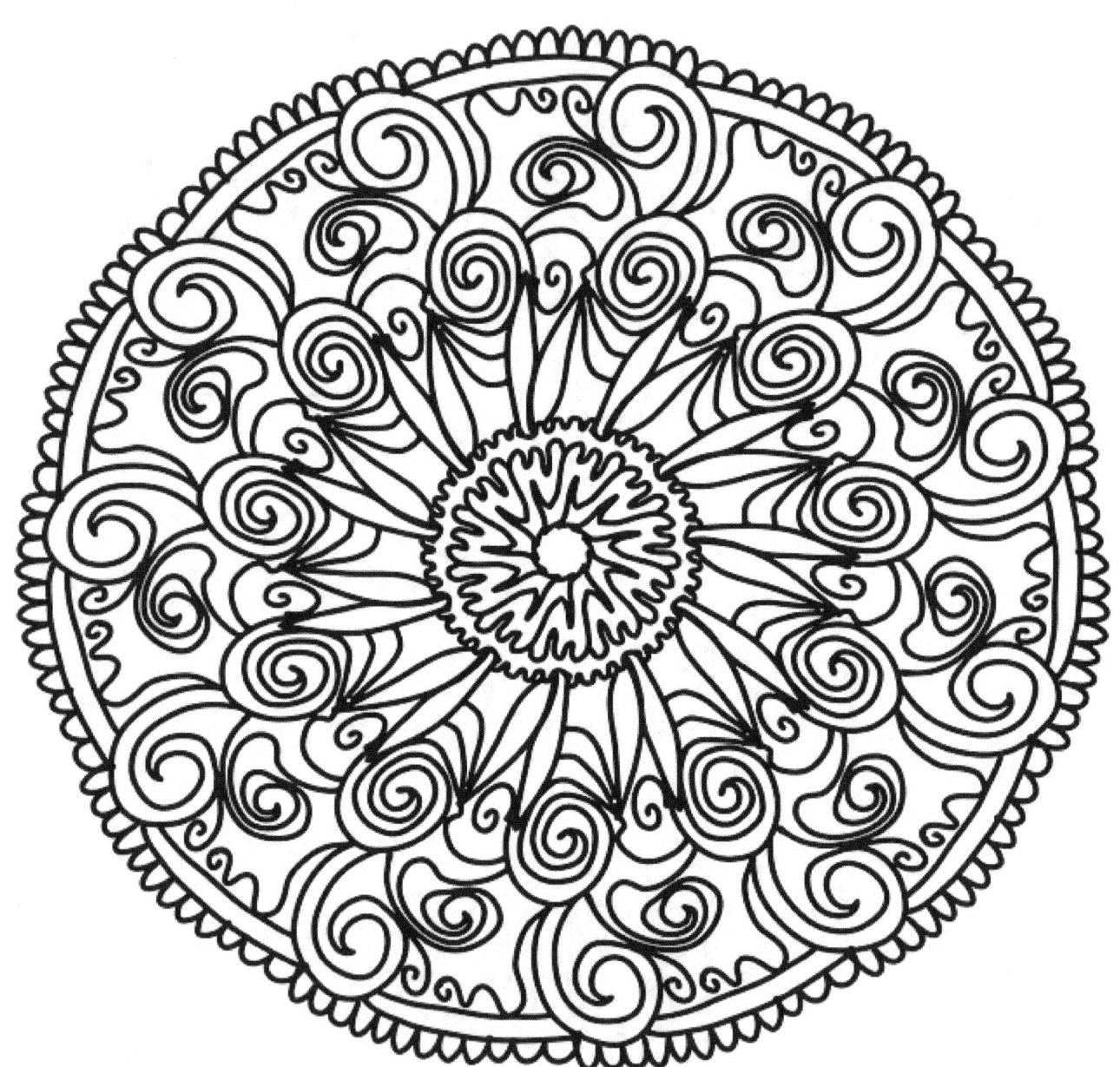

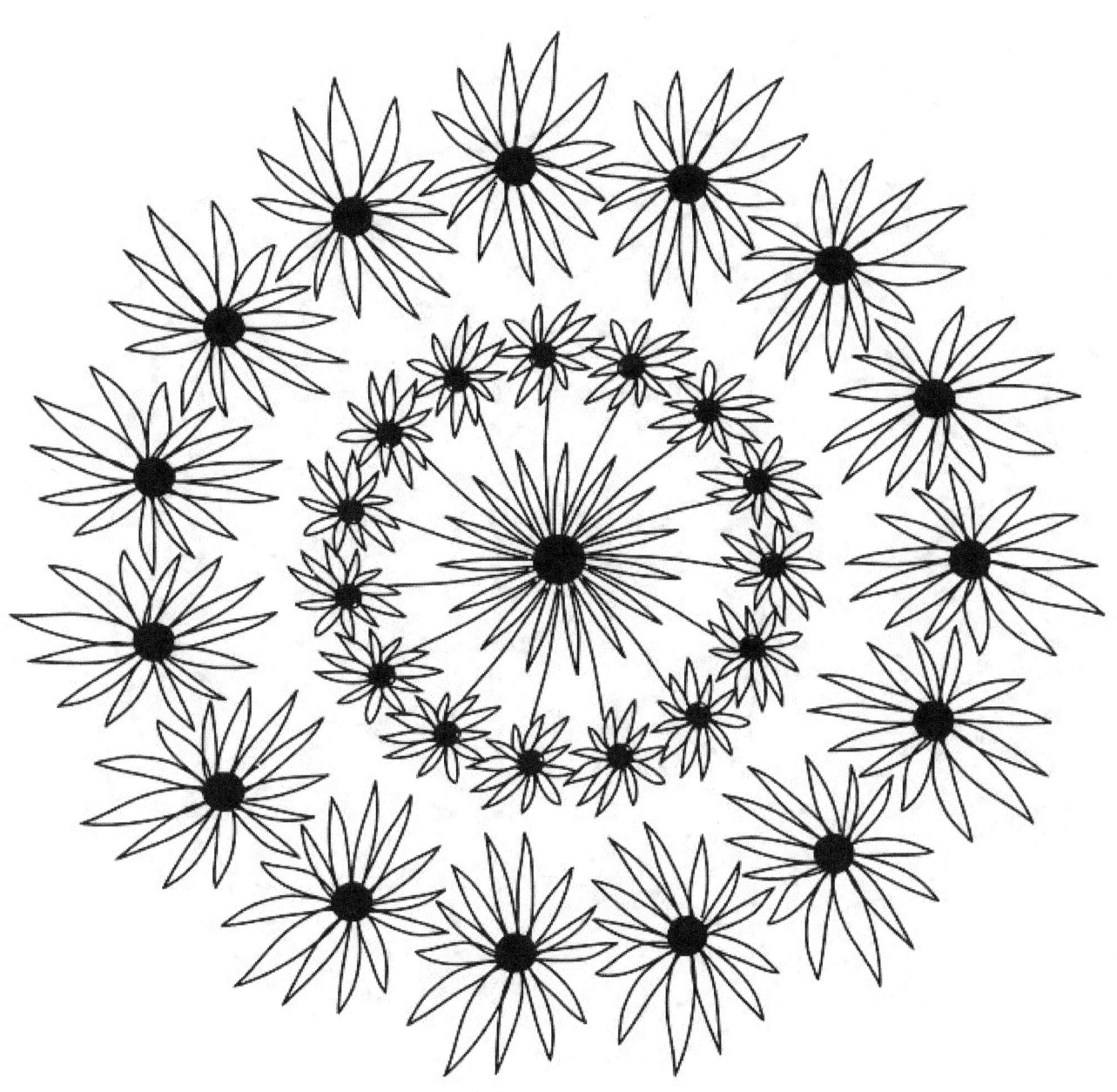

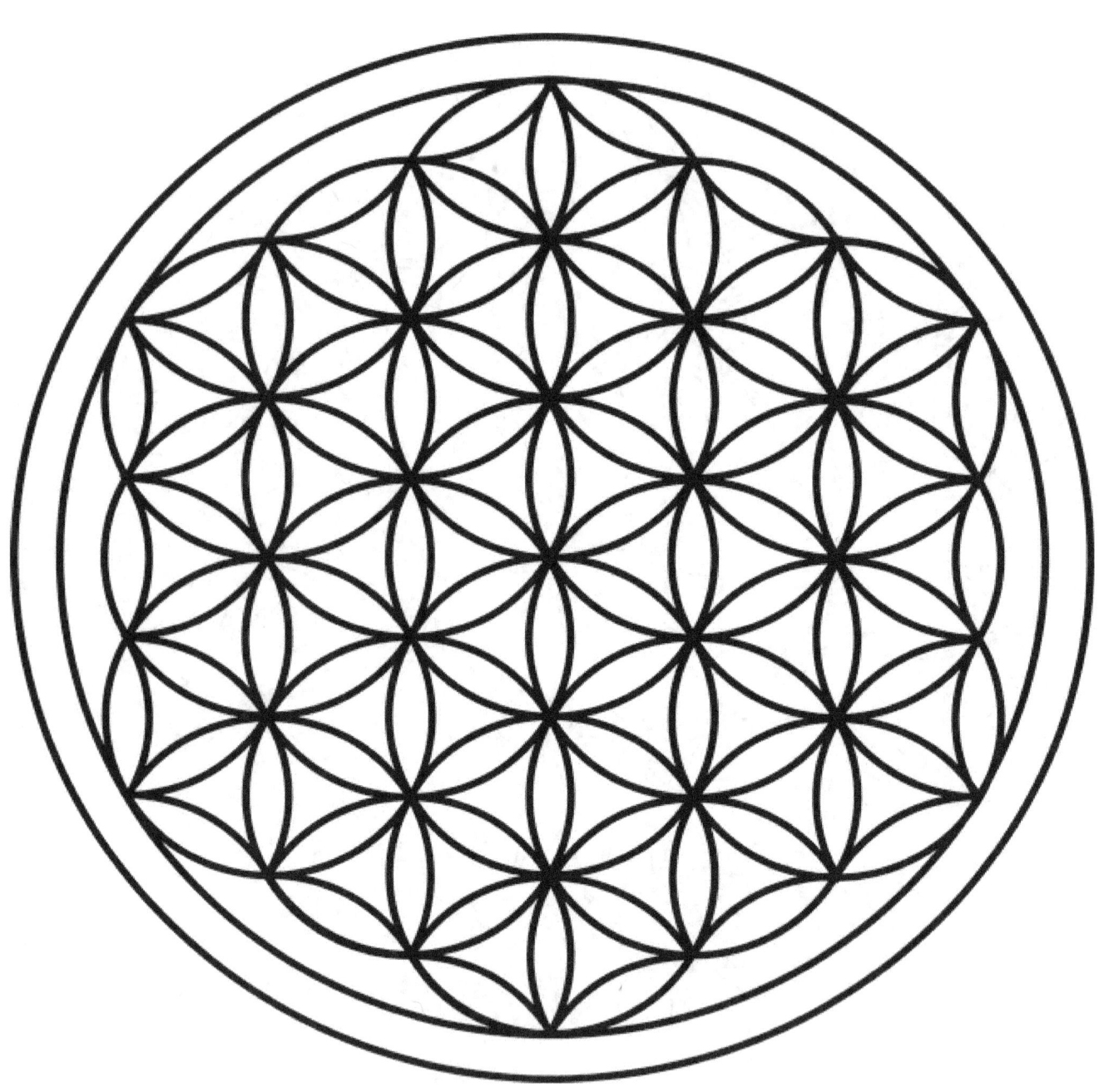

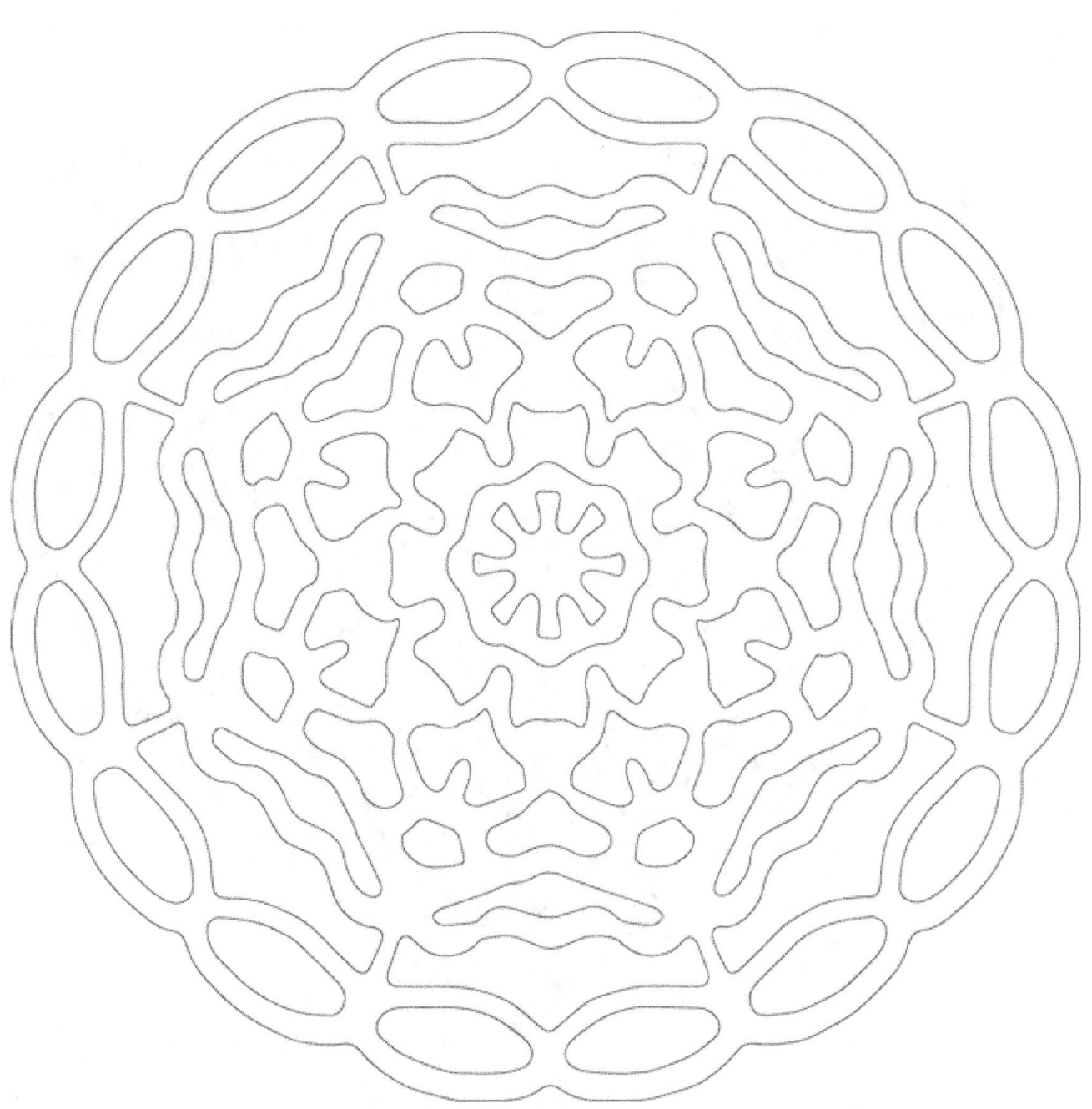

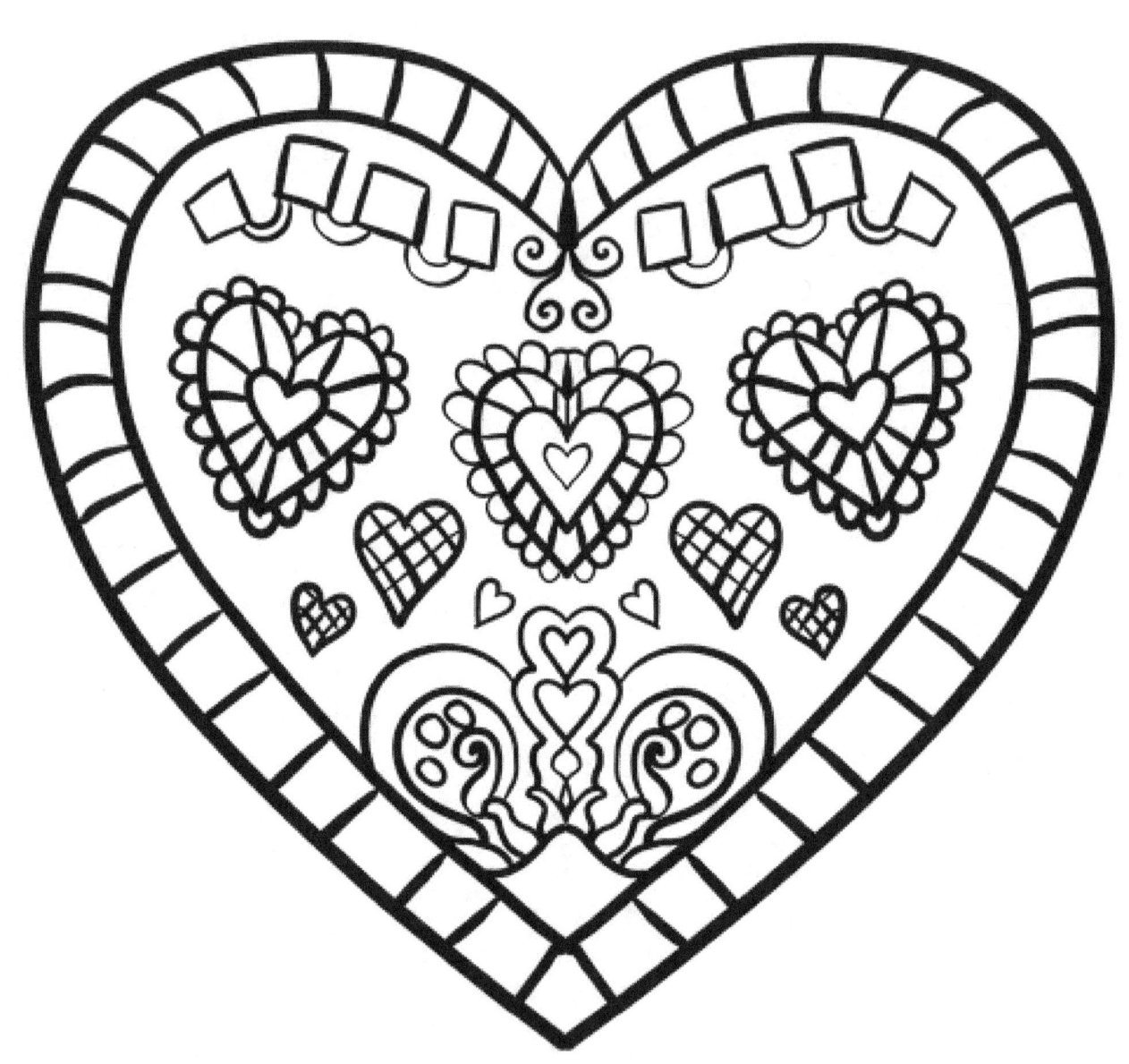

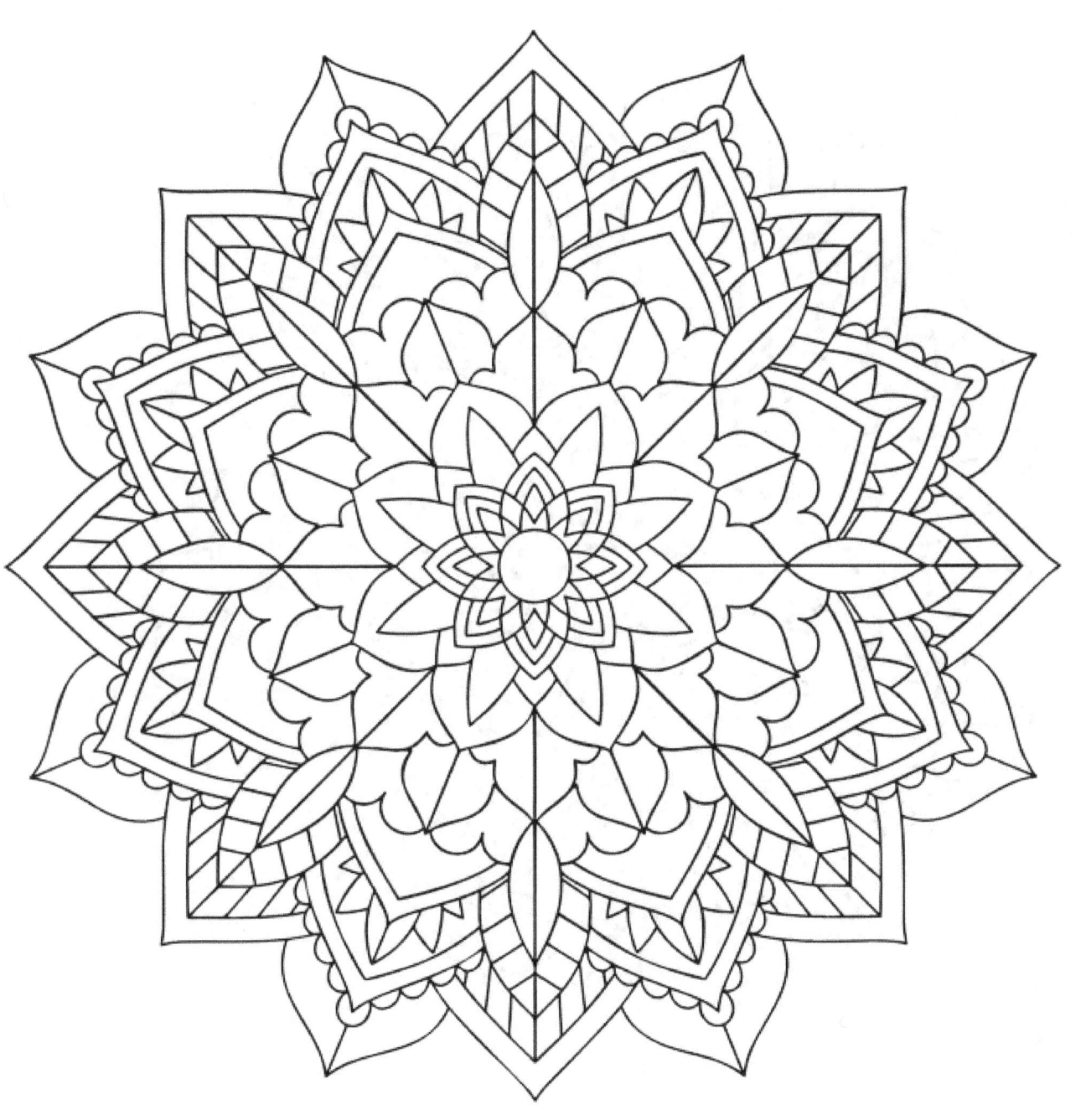

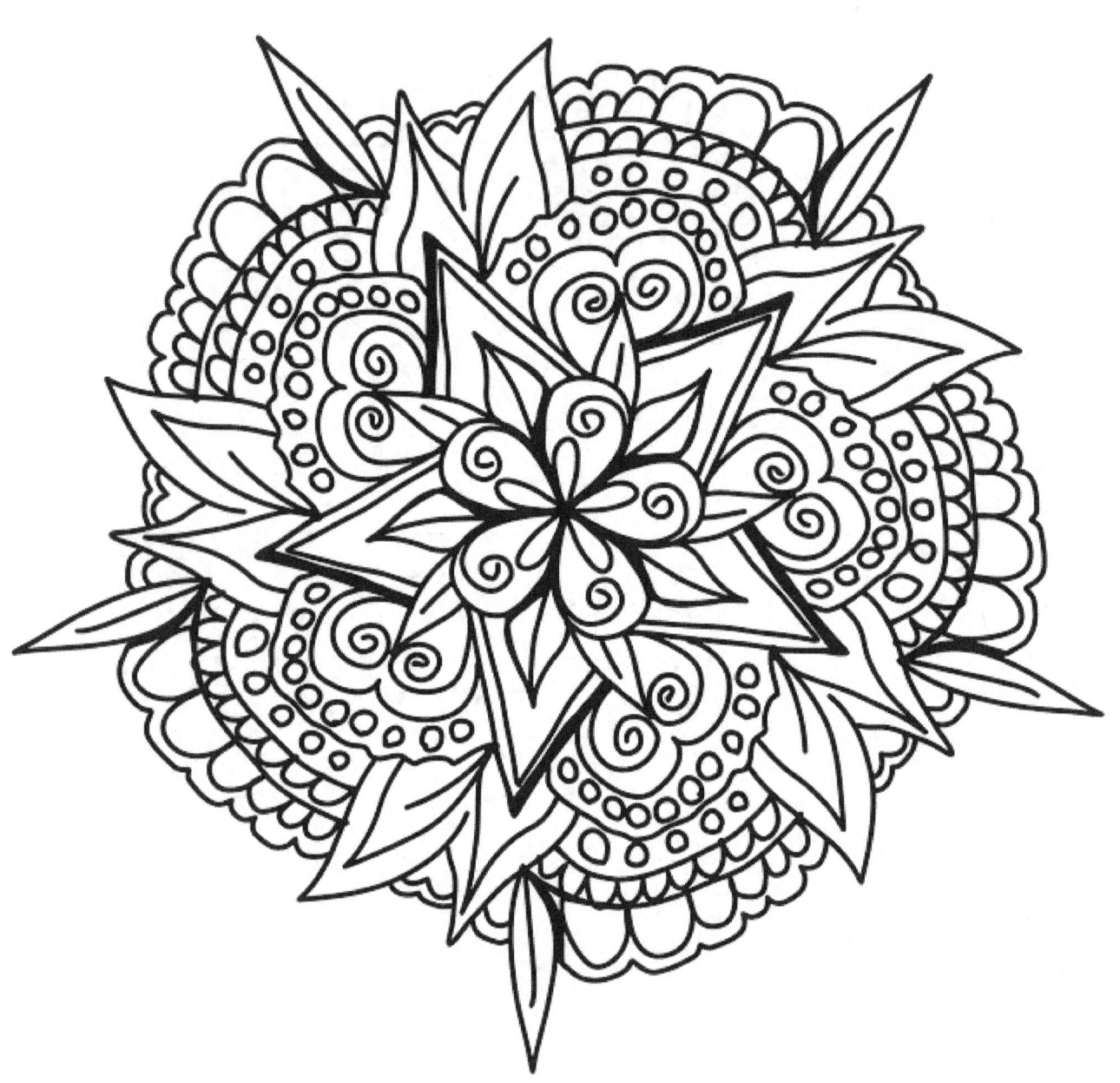

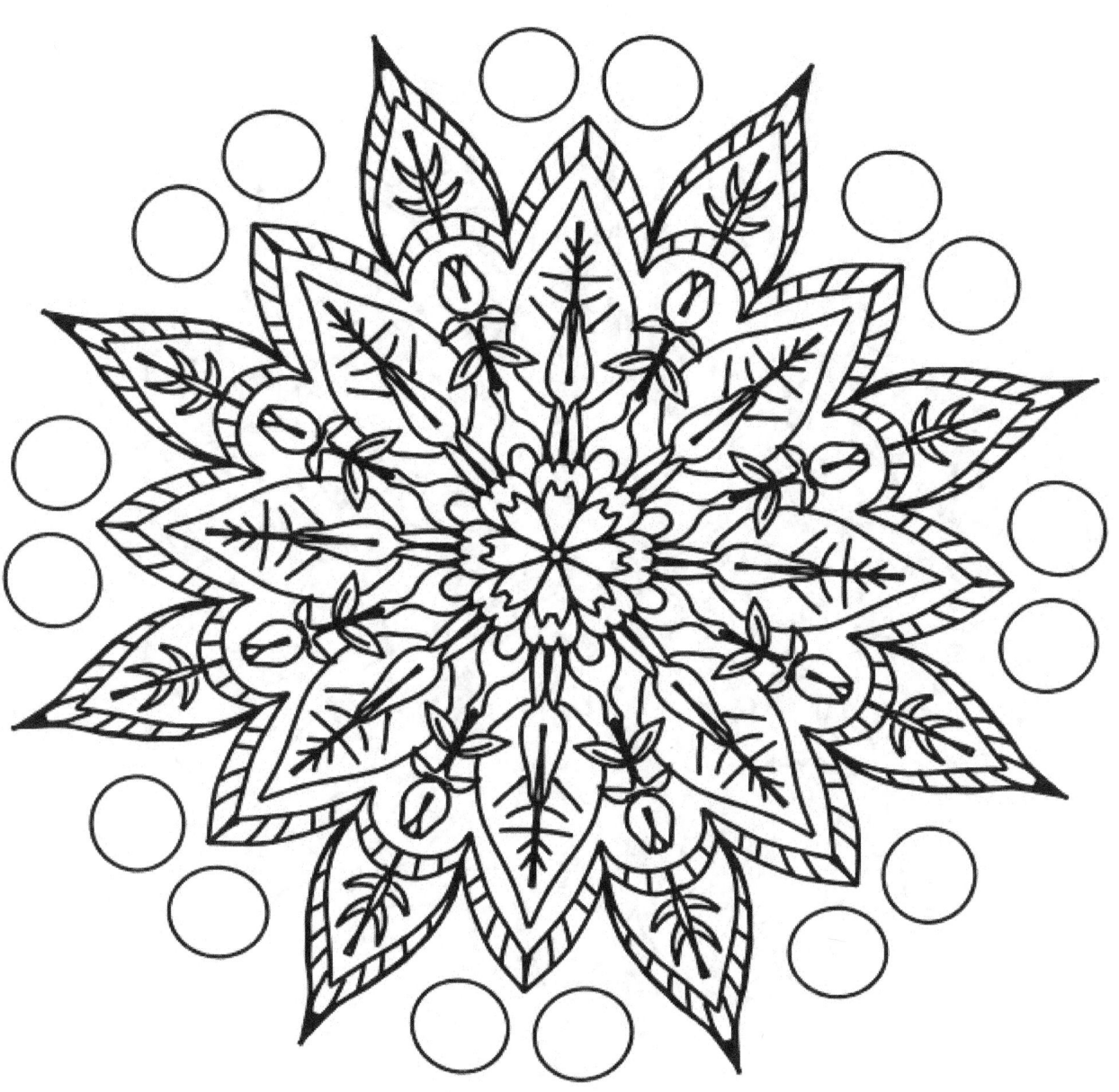

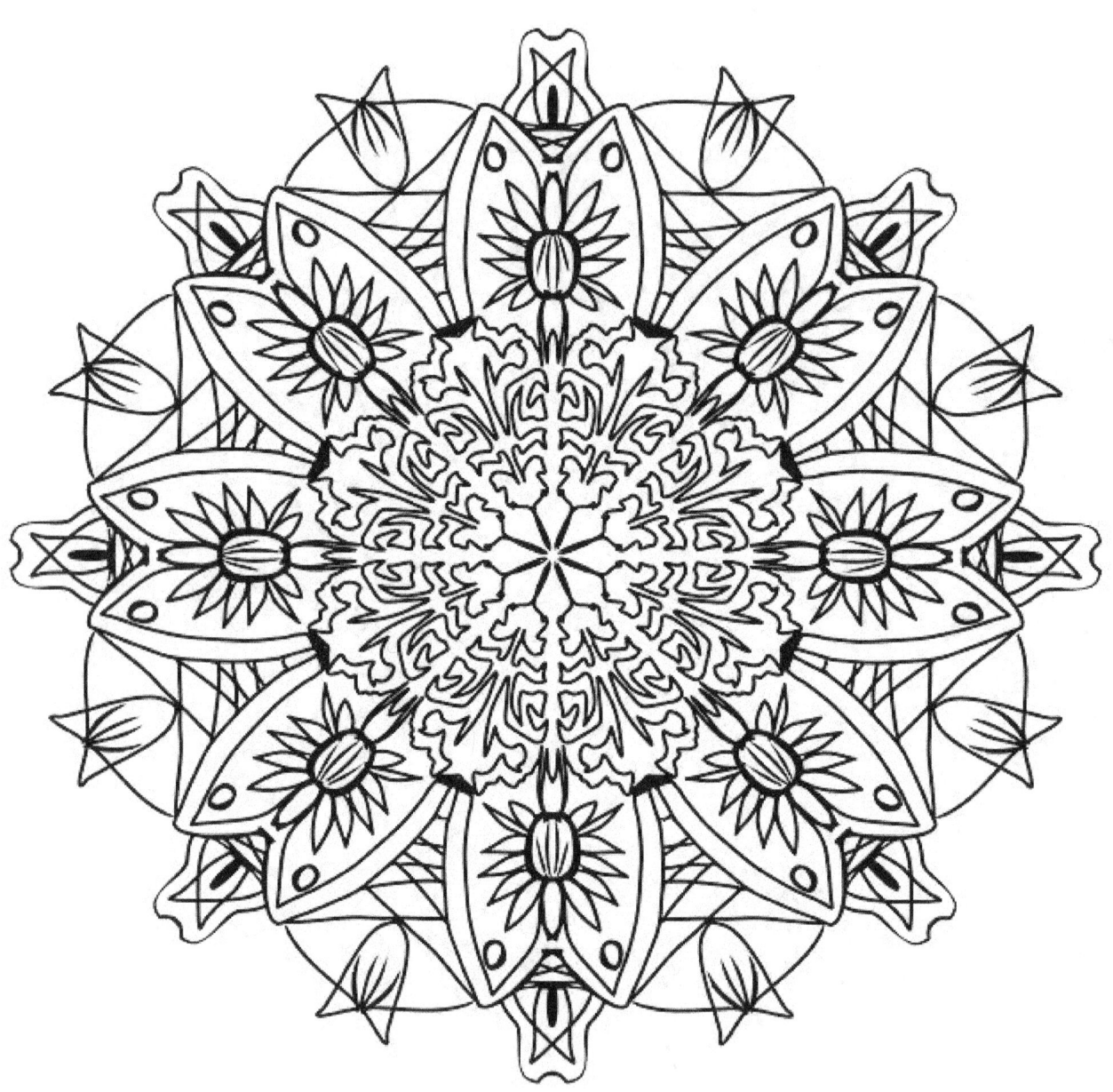

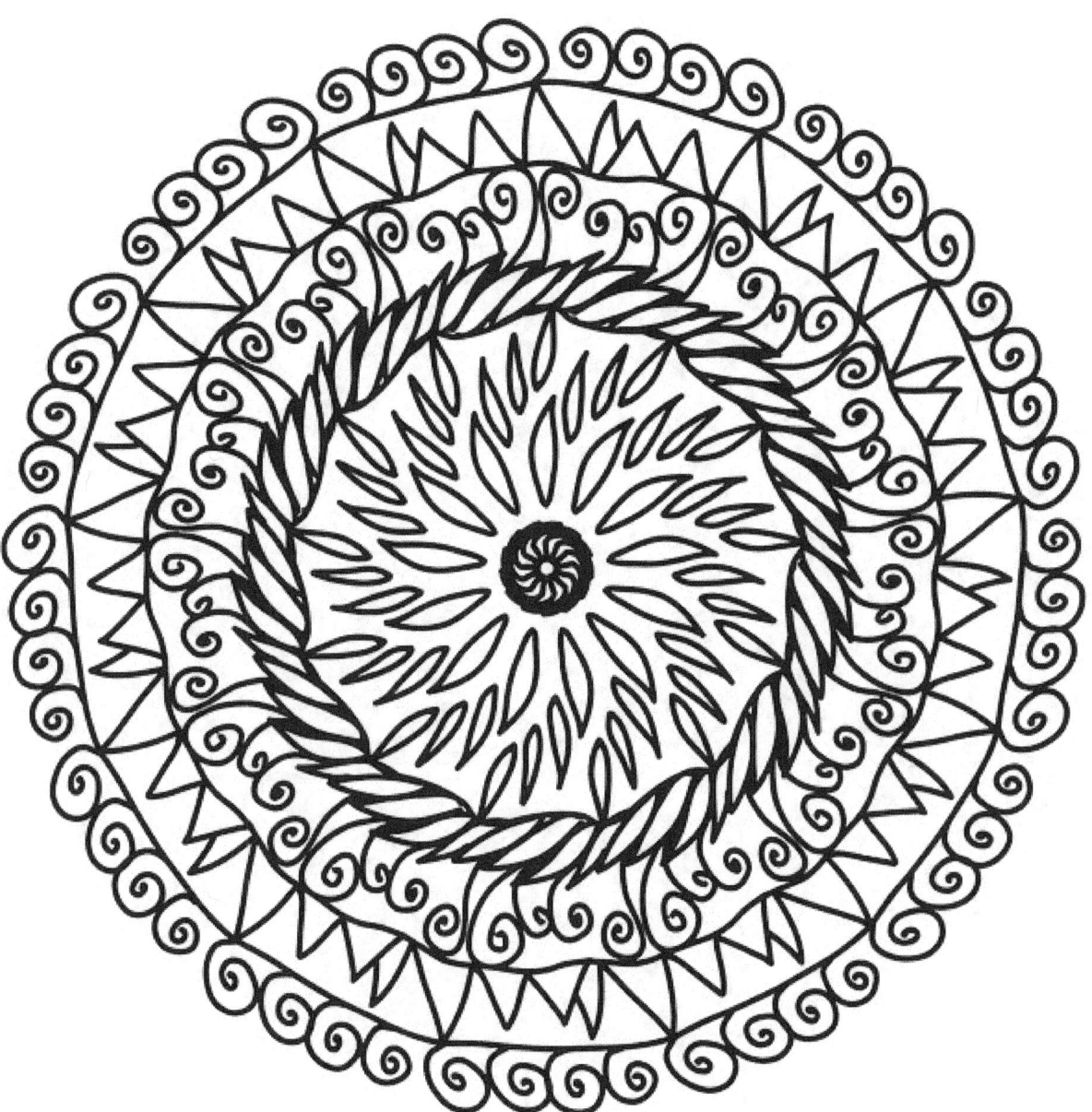

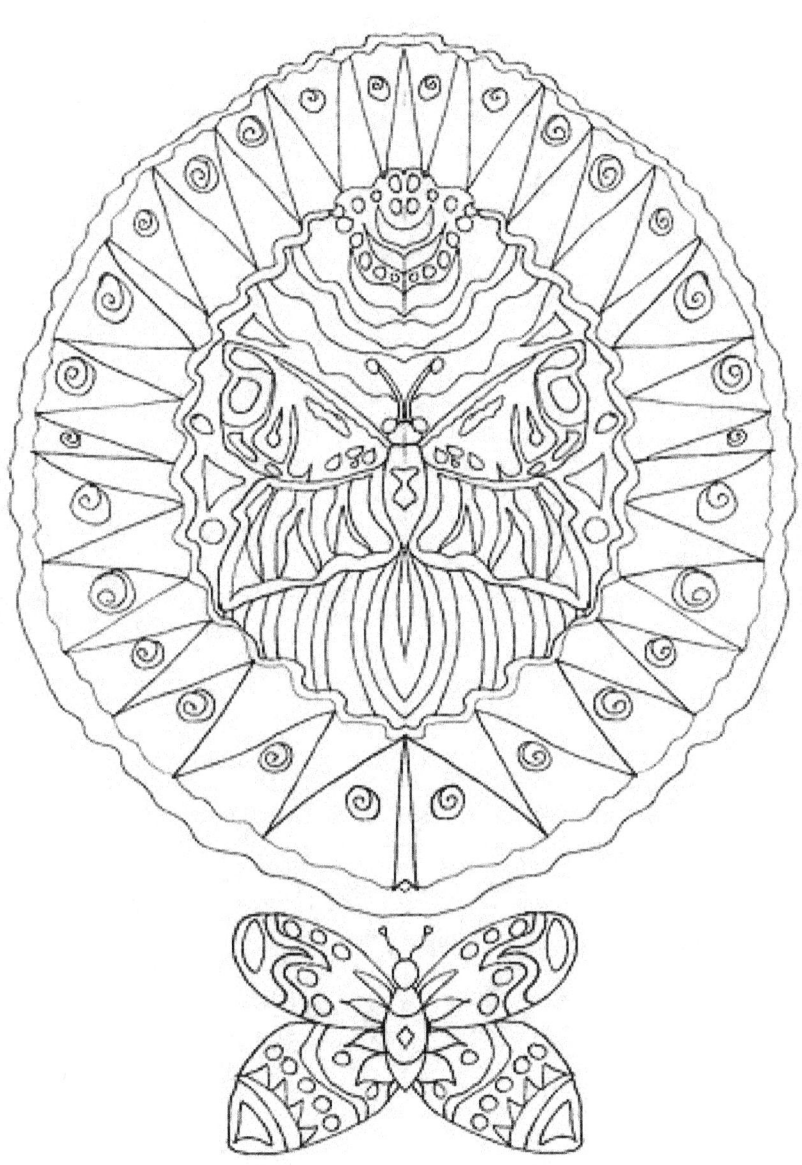

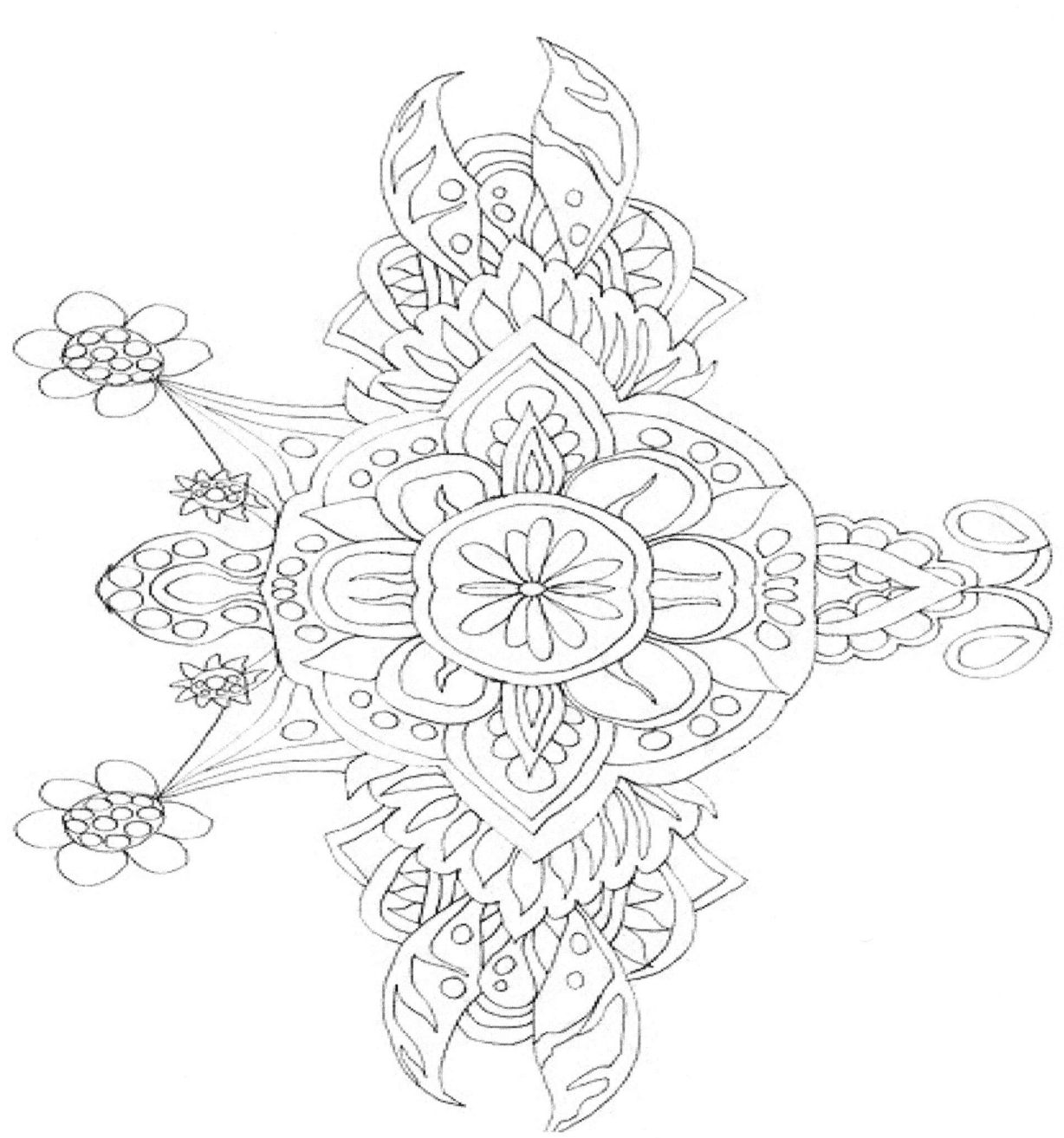

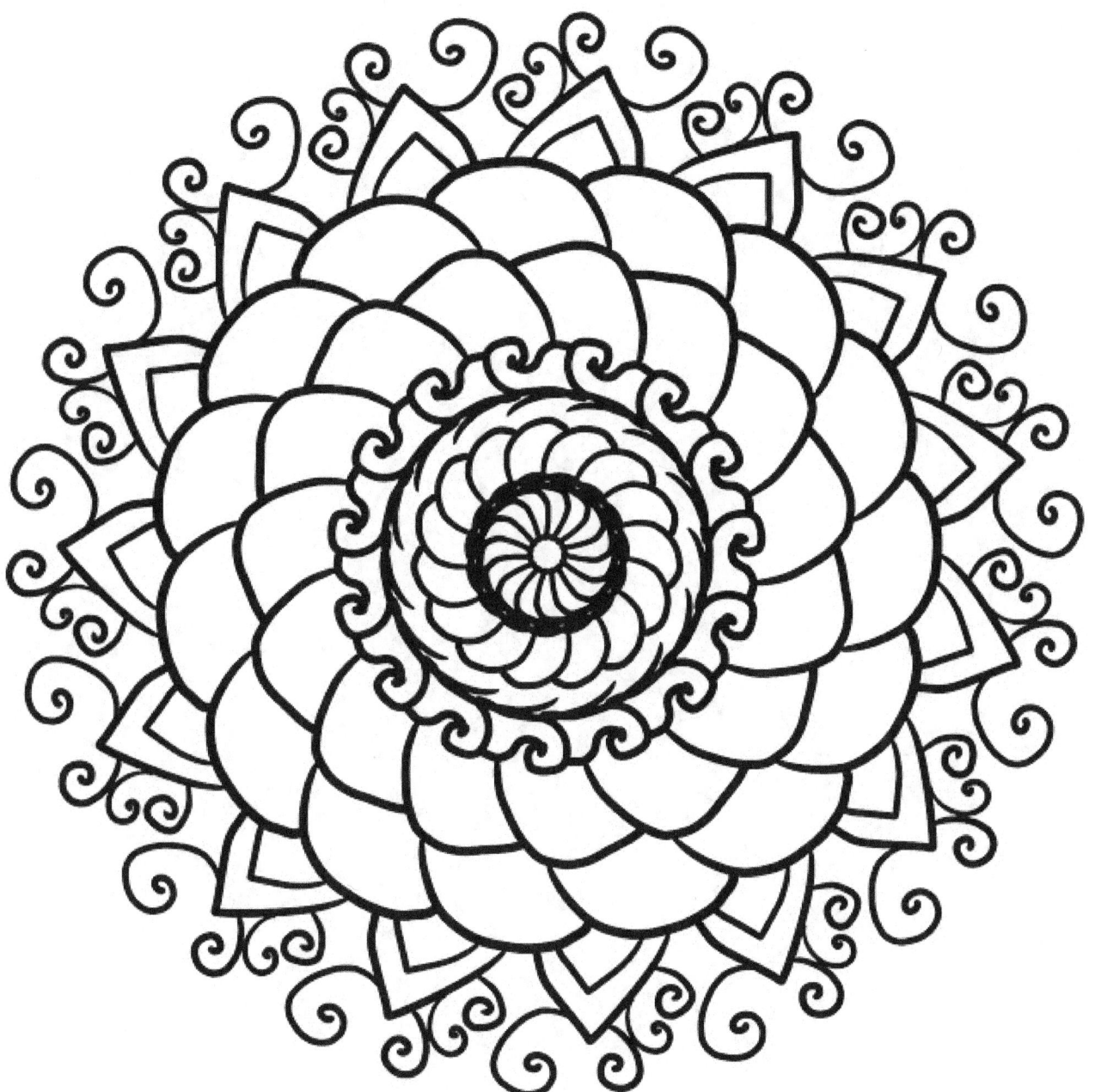

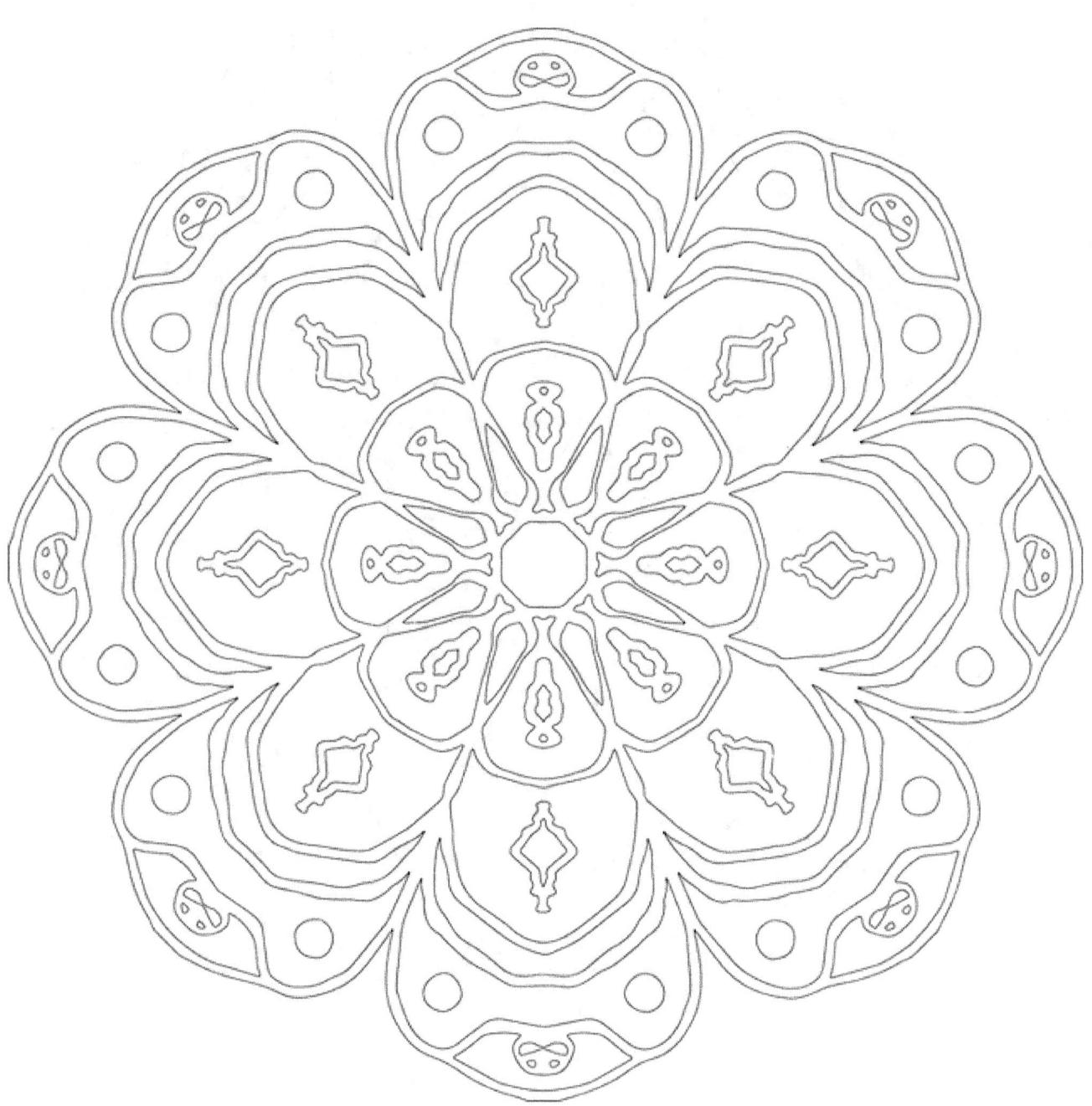

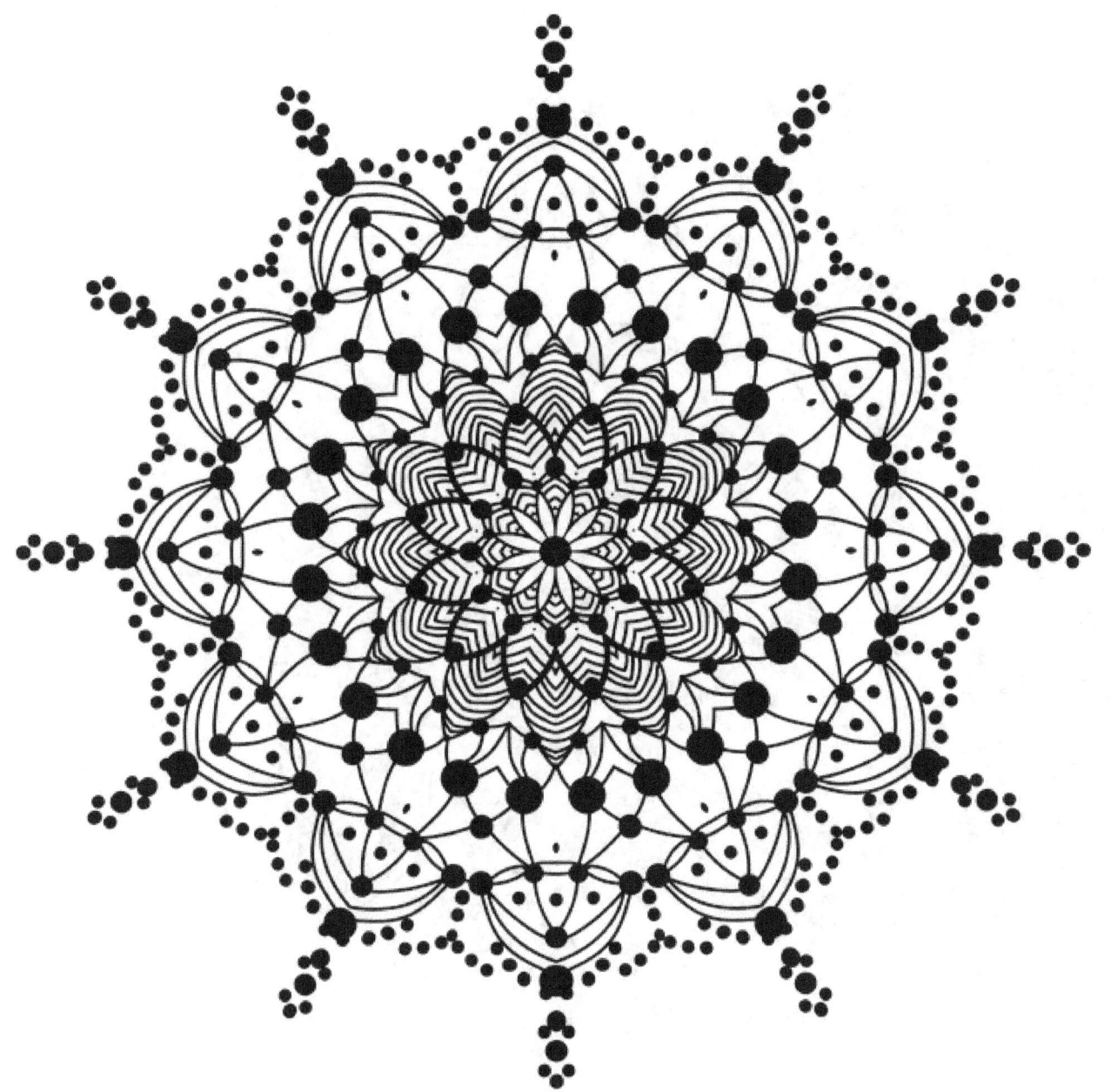

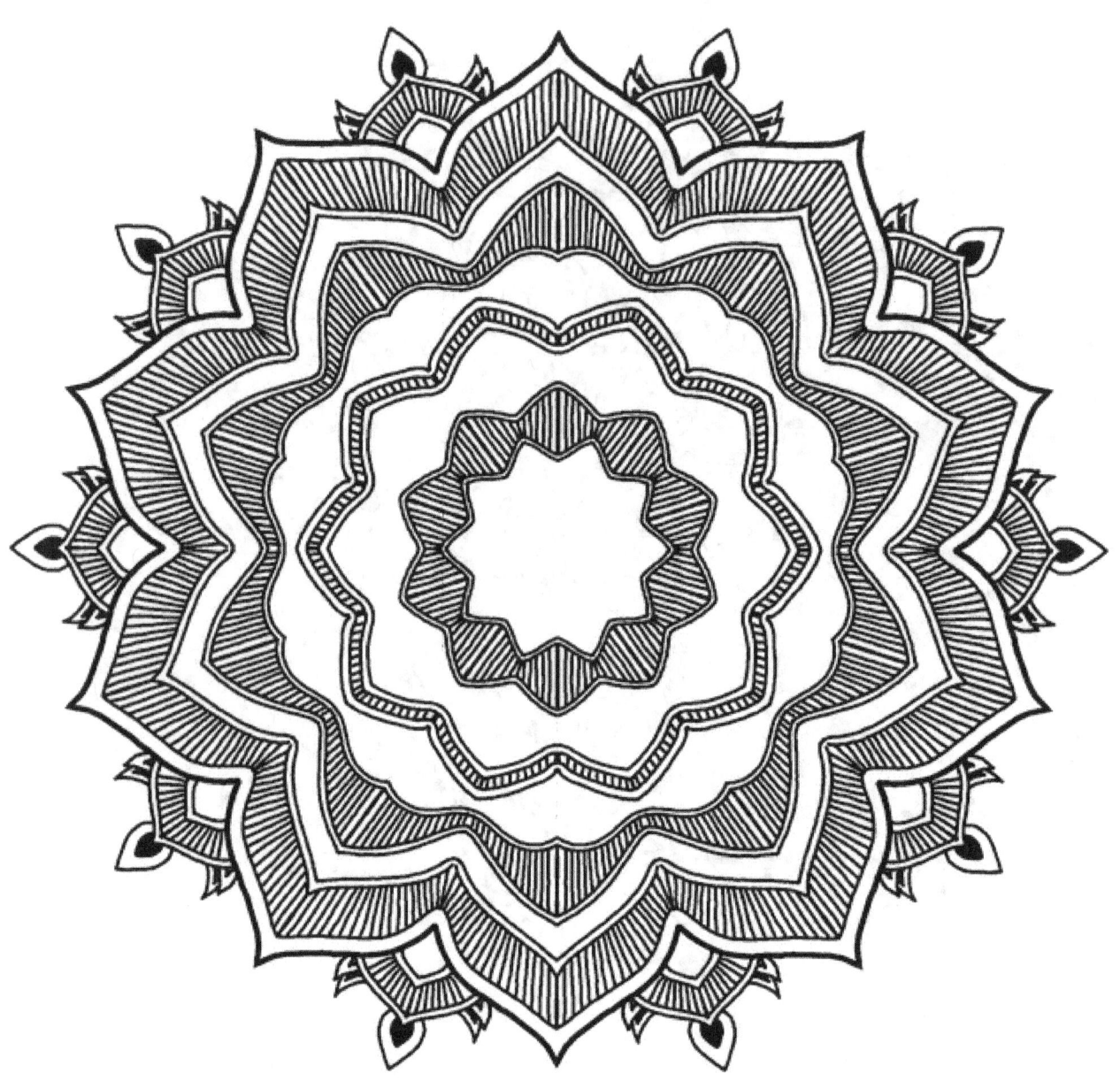

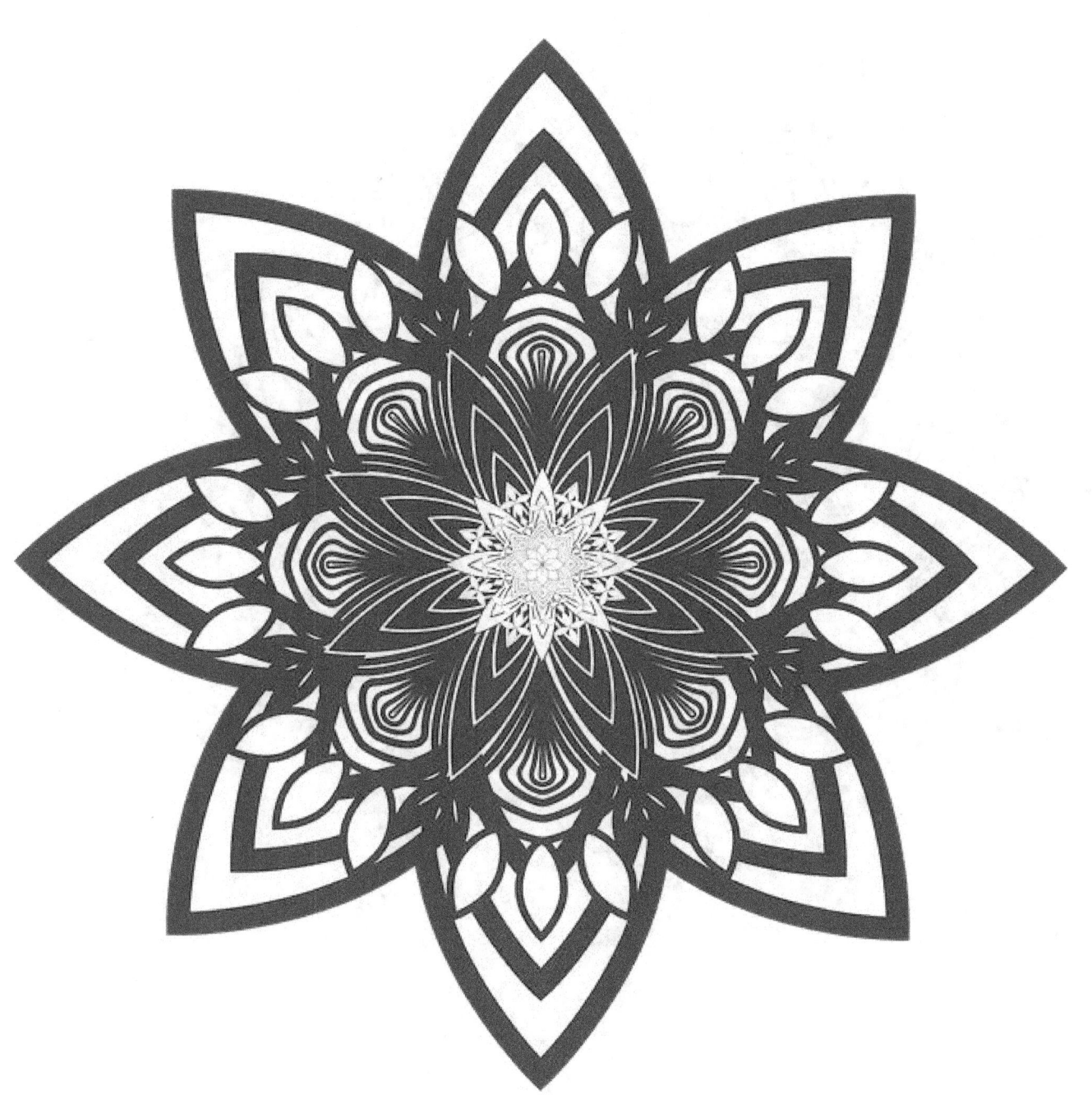

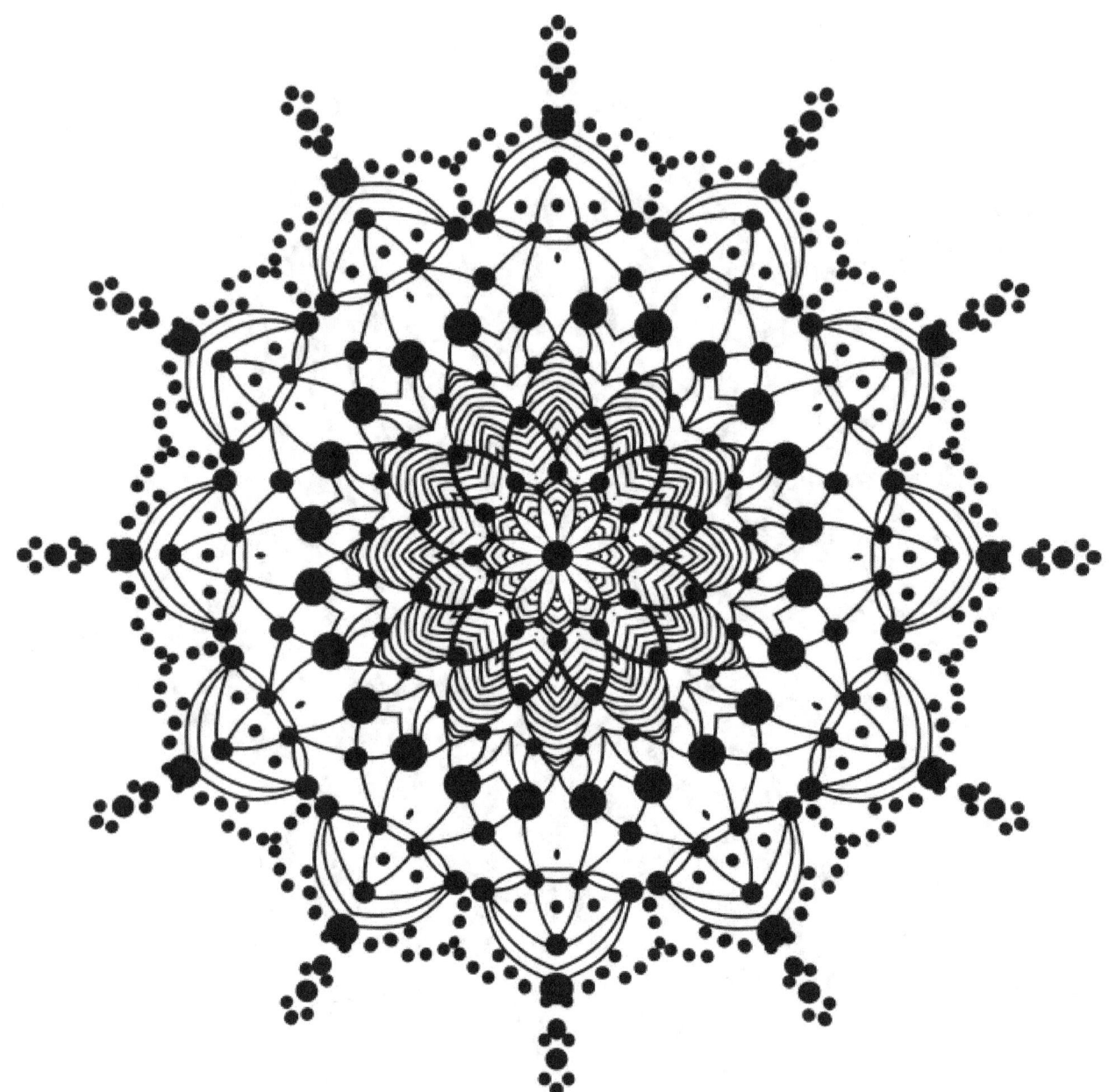